T0098255

The

Human Biological

Machine

—— as a ——

Transformational

Apparatus

The
Human Biological
Machine
—— as a ——
Transformational
Apparatus

E.J. Gold

Gateways Books and Tapes,
Nevada City, California

©2007 by E.J. Gold
Illustrations ©2007 by E.J. Gold
All Rights Reserved. Printed in the U.S.A.
First Printing: May 17, 1985
Second Printing: November 23, 1986
Third Printing: June 1, 1991
Second Edition: December, 2007
Published by: GATEWAYS/IDHHB, INC.
PO Box 370
Nevada City, CA 95959 (USA)
(800) 869-0658 or (530) 271-2239
http://www.gatewaysbooksandtapes.com
email: info@gatewaysbooksandtapes.com

ISBNs:
Trade Paperback: 978-0-89556-168-8
EPUB/Kindle: 978-0-89556-432-0
Mobipocket: 978-0-89556-431-3
PDF: 978-0-89556-430-6

No part of this publication may be reproduced or transmitted in any
form or by any means, electronic or mechanical, including photocopy,
recording or any information storage and retrieval system now known or to
be invented, without permission in writing from the copyright holder,
except by a reviewer who wishes to quote brief passages in connection with
a review written for inclusion in a magazine, newspaper, or broadcast.

Library of Congress Cataloging-in-Publication Data
Gold, E. J.
The human biological machine as a transformational apparatus / E.J.
Gold. -- 2nd ed.
        p. cm.
Summary: "[Presents information and help on ways to unlock our full
transformational potential. An introduction to a large body of work by
EJ Gold in the field of transformationl psychology]"--Provided by
publisher.
ISBN-13: 978-0-89556-168-8
1. Occultism. 2. Institute for the Development of the Harmonious
Human Being. I. Title.
BF1999.G6216 2007
131--dc22
                    2007046915

Table of Contents

The purpose of beginning work is to bring the machine into the waking state and to enable it to function as a transformational apparatus. Transformation is not an aim in itself but a stepping stone to a whole new way of life which we seek.

Because the machine—although fully functional in the ordinary sense—lives its whole life in the sleeping state, our work begins in sleep. We must learn to use the elements of sleep to overcome the machine's defense mechanism against the waking state.

By making our formulation of our inner aims toward transformation more exact, we may eventually develop a real work aim, not something mental and subjective, but an aim which is practical, immediate, accomplishable and which could actually serve a greater, more objective aim.

Although we are separate from the machine, we have become hypnotized, immersed in the sleeping state of the machine. One of the purposes of studying the machine is to gather evidence which can help us define the exact nature of this sleep.

The human biological machine is a powerful dominant electrical field which can, if its transformational functions are activated by the waking state, act electrically upon the essential self . . . another, less powerful but more subtle electrical field which forms the true self.

Because life experiences—mnemonically stored in the muscles of the body—have distorted the electrical field of the machine, repair of these anomalies in the general electrical field are necessary in order for the machine to function effectively as a transformational apparatus.

Information in the evolutionary sense is transmitted by impingement of one electrical field upon another. The electrical field of the essential self undergoes the exact change necessary to free it from its compulsive electrical affinity for the human biological machine.

Real help is not someone doing something for us, or a lessening of our personal suffering and struggles. Real help has no calming effect—quite the contrary—it makes the machine squirm itself into evolution-by-reflex.

Alchemy is not a way of producing behavioral change in the machine; it is a way of notating change that occurs on a much deeper level. It is not a cause, but an effect, a reflection of the inner evolution of the essential self.

If we follow the machine as a lover would, unrelentingly fixing his gaze upon his Beloved, filled with astonishment, rapture and gratitude, the machine will come to life, awakening and responding to the power of adoration with a profound emotion which will in turn bring about our own transformation.

In our beginning work, we often attempt to accomplish too much at once. Our efforts are scattered and our energy quickly dissipates itself. We must discipline ourselves to improve the quality and potency of our efforts by condensing them at first.

Growth of the soul requires a form of human sacrifice, the exact nature of which has long since been distorted in mainstream thought. Evolutionary barriers—flaws in the diamond—are ground down by abrasion.

Once we are able to bring the machine to stillness and silence, we will experience ourselves as definitely separate from the machine with a life apart from and far beyond the life of the machine.

Because of its fear of not being able to reintegrate the sleeping state, the machine has learnt to defend itself against the waking state. Each individual has a particular defense mechanism called the Chronic which is triggered off whenever the machine is threatened with awakening.

The relationship between the essential self and the machine is based on a seduction, an affinity—electrical in nature—between their electrical fields. Evolution thus means transformation of the electrical field of the essential self in such a way as to free it from this affinity.

By constantly restimulating areas of charge in the electrical field of the machine, we are able to clear it of its ridges and eddies which impinge on the electrical field of the essential self.

The quest for the permanent vision of the higher dimension may strike us as odd, but we must understand how the vision of another world—even without knowing much about it—would change us and bring about our certain transformation.

The following is an account of an experience which Janet, a medical doctor located in New York City, had with her chronic and how she was able to use it to cross into the waking state.

Foreword

E.J. Gold has hit the nail squarely on the head. *Man is an unfinished animal endowed by nature with the capacity to complete itself.* It can then take charge of its own evolution and become worthy of the proud title *Homo sapiens.* The alchemical process of self-completion is shrouded in mystery and understood only by a few people in each generation. The Great Work consists in transforming a helpless other-directed puppet into an inner-directed, unified being that understands its place in the scheme of things. Nothing can be more important than the attainment of this understanding. Without it we are at the mercy of our dreams and delusions and our technical devices become more of a menace than a blessing. If a great catastrophe is to be avoided, a growing number of people must grasp the central truth. To complete one's own inner transformation is the only task worth taking seriously. Everything else is secondary.

Robert S. de Ropp
author of *The Master Game*

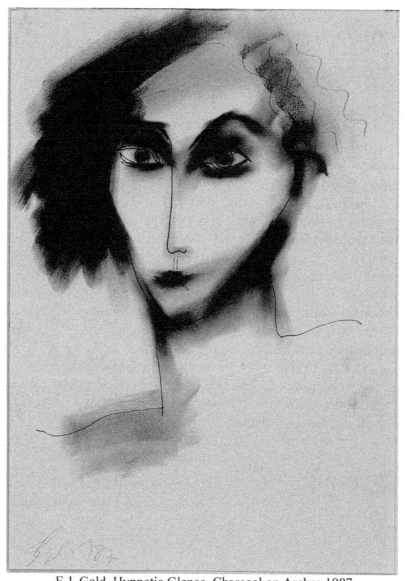

E.J. Gold, Hypnotic Glance, Charcoal on Arches 1987

Introduction

(This is a transcription of a talk given at a special workshop)

I've been passing on a lot of information over the past three-and-a-half billion years – since Thursday, and these are some of my notes. These are just the high points, as it were.

This all came about actually from a question that was asked, not in my presence. The question was raised, "Gee, what do you do with the waking state, in the waking state?" First, I'm not calling the not-waking-state the sleep state. I don't like the term the sleep state, because it's not exactly right. So I've decided to call it the "napping" state, which is closer. It's not right, nothing's exactly right, but it's closer to what I mean. So I'm calling it the napping state. To lie down, take a little nappy state. But you might be standing and napping. It's different from sleeping, because sleeping implies that you're actually regenerating something, that you're deep, deep, deep in the subconscious levels. That's not necessarily true. Napping is a very light state of sleep, and that's what I mean. It's a somnambulant state. It's a state where you can carry on business as usual.

You can drive down a freeway and then wake up from it, and you don't have to wake up entirely. You just wake up a little bit from it, and now you're in the ordinary napping state.

You can go into very deep levels of sleep when you're driving to such an extent that you have no idea where you've been for the past hour. But that's not the napping state that you normally experience. The napping state you normally experience is one where you seem to be awake, but you are not actually awake. What does *awake* mean? First of all, if you're going to talk about the "waking state", you must identify it as a very specific state. Otherwise, it's just this kind of amorphous blob of stateness, which is not the same thing as "a state."

Let's get very specific about what we mean by a waking state. There are a number of games that I've invented over the past four days or so that can be played, which will assist both in achieving the waking state and also at working within, or inside, the waking state – actually tolerating and working in the waking state. The waking state is to be truly awake. That means to be completely, utterly, absolutely aware, with all the senses of reality, meaning that you actually are in that space that we all know about, that space where we are *truly awake*.

Again, what does *awake* mean? You get the concatenation of everything all at once. You're at the highest possible level of consciousness for you. Everyone achieves some sort of waking state at the limit of their tolerance. The waking state that we're after is just a little past your level of tolerance where it's almost too much, but not quite. The sensations, the thoughts, the feelings, the concepts, the knowingness, the wisdom – whatever it might be that falls upon you in the waking state – that is the waking state that we're after, for you. The nifty thing is that the waking state has gradations, and that each individual achieves some measure of waking state according to their tolerance for eternity, infinity and the "other thing." The other thing is the thing that you know what I mean, but we never speak of it. When you're in that state, you know exactly what I'm talking about – that other thing – infinity, eternity, and the other thing.

So when you can sit in that space, that's the waking state that you can achieve at the moment. You're working, obviously, to extend that. When you begin consciously working on yourself, you're remembering yourself, which is re-membering, assembling, re-assembling yourself, putting yourself back together into the waking state. Right now, you're spattered all over the universe. You're going to be re-assembling yourself into the waking state. The waking state – you take as much responsibility for Godness as you can possibly manage. You let yourself be God as much as you possibly can. Maybe that's very little, maybe that's a lot, doesn't matter, doesn't make any difference at all – what you can do is what you can do. No one asked you to do anything beyond the limit of what you can do.

Why do that at all? Why not just let one take that full responsibility? The answer is *pain* – anguish, actually. And so we are learning to take some of that responsibility, some of that burden. Let's call it "the great burden." Take some of the great burden upon ourselves, even if only momentarily, or for a short period of time, or for a long period of time; it's all subjective because time doesn't actually exist in that space. So, sharing that burden, there is a network of sharers of that burden. That network is called the Great Work: those who share the great burden of Godness, of Absoluteness. Learning to share your portion of that is part of the conscious act that you perform in this work, coming here. That's what you're really here to do is to learn how to take some portion of that. The price you must pay for that is to sacrifice your aloneness in the highest space.

To sacrifice your own personal suffering as the Absolute, all alone. You must *share* the burden if you wish the burden to be shared. You have to give up some of the responsibility in order to get some of the load off you. Otherwise, like the average obsessive/compulsive, you *can't let go* of any single shred of responsibility *to anyone* for any reason. That's just on an ordinary level, just in a work space. "No, I can't let you do that! You might do it wrong!" If you can't let go on that level, you surely can't let go on the Absolute level. And share – let some of that happen.

There are a variety of methods employed in the sharing of that burden. There are a number of, let's call it, enclaves, or packs of green (POG). They are networked *together* and they work together to share that burden, and also, of course, to pass on the technique, the method, of sharing that burden.

(Light went off briefly) Thank you. Ah! I thought it was something much greater than somebody leaning against the light switches. You know, obviously, there's a coincidence there. As you leaned against the light switch, the lights went out. There is no actual connection between those things, but we're trained to think there was. Makes things a lot easier to take than suddenly the lights went out, and then she leaned against the thing to explain it. Some of us think life's a bit like that.

Actually what the waking state does is it brings to an end your napping cycle. It brings to *an* end – not *the* end – your dream, the dream you're dreaming right now. It brings that to an end. And in order to achieve, even momentarily, the waking state, which is all you're going to try to do is just get one *moment* of waking state – just a single *glimpse* at it. You're not going to try to hang out in there – that's very unwise at this time.

You need to learn the Zen Clap in order to get to play this particular game. I'm not going to go into a whole lot of theory at this point. I'm just going to show you how the game is played. Then it's up to you. It's your own responsibility whether you play the game or cheat the game. In order to play the game, you must absolutely, without fail, go into the waking state, awaken, at the clap of your hands, on a particular question.

The question was asked, "What do you do once you're in the waking state?" I accepted that question only because it was asked out of ignorance. And the reason it was asked out of ignorance is because the asker did not have enough background to ask the correct question from that. It's sort of an implied question, but it isn't actually directly asked. And that's the failure of any question in any serious way. How precise is the question? How good is the question? Because the question will be a determinant factor with the answer. In other words, the answer to the question is only as good as the question was specific. Otherwise, you get "42", and you have no idea what the question was.

The question should be asked, "What do I do once I have *achieved* the waking state?" or "What do I do *with* the waking state?" "What *can* I do with the waking state?" is another way of asking it. "What can I do with the *waking* state?"

So, I'm going to clap my hands, and when I clap my hands, I want you to just flicker into the waking state for a moment, and then notice an answer there if you can get one. So, you're all going to ask, "What can I do with the waking state?" Right, together. (Everyone all at once says:) "What can I do with the waking state?"

Now you're going to say this with me, "Let's find out *now*." Ready? And we'll clap our hands. And now you're going to wake up! Everyone say it again, "What can I do with the waking state?" Everyone together say: "Let's find out . . . (clapping hands at the same time and saying:) *now!*"

You just flick into it and out of it, just for a moment. Now you're going to try to stay there longer obviously. Don't cling to it. Just let it go by. We're going to start working with practical exercises in the waking state, practical exercises to induce it. That's your practical exercise, to induce it right there. I dare you to enter the waking state. What can I do with the waking state? Let's find out . . . (clapping hands at the same time while saying:) . . . *now!* Not later, not sometime in the future, not tell me about it. Go into the waking state and see what you do, see how you behave, see how you act, see what you do, see what happens. Because there really is no other answer for it other than to be in the waking state, and then take a look at it.

I have to do that when I do editing. I've got to go into the video game orb and walk around in there to see what has happened. Then I make a change here, a change there, and I take a look at it. You've got to go into the waking state to take a look at, to see the procedure, to see what's happening. How is it proceeding? How is your work going in the waking state?

I don't know, I'm not in it. Speculating without a speculum. It's useless.

So we're going to talk, first of all, explore, and I'm not going to do this all today because clearly, it's just not possible. But I'll give you some of the notes to work with. We're going to work with practical exercises in the waking state. We're going to learn how to tolerate the waking state and work within it, to your level of tolerance. Nobody else's – yours.

One of the techniques that we are developing is to work as a group, a team, a pack of green. That is with the idea in mind that we are all sharing a single burden. Each in our own way, we're sharing a single burden. We're all taking some responsibility for that burden. Now, as you take responsibility back to yourself, you're losing the hypnotic state. Hypnosis means to give away responsibility. When you're with a hypnotist, the hypnotist is taking responsibility away from you, and you're willingly giving, fool that you are, because you're living in what's called the "chimp zone."

The chimp zone is the monkey space, the monkey area. That's where you normally live is in the chimp zone. Chimps don't like responsibility. They'll look around and see who to copy, who to imitate, whose robe to touch. So you want to move away from, at least, the chimp state to the chump state, which is: "Why me?" That's the one where you feel the burden the most. You say, "How come I get the burden the worst? Everybody else has an easy, cool way to handle the burden. I have to do it this way." Everyone feels that. They all feel like they've been shunned, that they've been suckered.

That's just a state that you pass through when you've first taken responsibility back to yourself for Godness, for

Absoluteness. You start feeling like a chump, like you've been suckered. It's like the sergeant who goes over the top and looks back, and there's nobody back there. "Come on, let's go – charge! Hey! I'm being shot at. I'm the only one out here." So you feel like a chump. And then go from there to the champ state, which is where you say, "I made it. I'm feeling good about myself." And, then you move past that into other, even more exalted states than that.

Now, there is a price to pay. I mentioned it earlier. The price that you pay is your personalness, your personal loneliness, your loneliness at the top. It's lonely at the top, only if you're alone at the top. If there's a sharing of that burden, then you won't feel that. But that's the box you live in, for God's sake. So, the very box you live in is the box you have to dismantle there. You've got to open up the walls, and just open the thing up and go to the limits of creation, right to the boundary of creation, that boundary where creation is actually expanding out, and it's happening. It's at that very boundary, the boundary of creation, the crowning of creation, the crown of creation. That's where all the walls are the total size of the universe. This is as far as we can get it. This is as far as it goes. We'll take down the walls, push them out a bit . . . push them out a bit more . . . get a little bit bigger, and start expanding out from your little hovel, and expand out a little bit into the map, into the universal map. Get out there. Take responsibility for more and more.

Oh, this is a paranoid's delight, you see. In the ultimate space . . . the ultimate . . . space . . . it's normal to be paranoid. You have to be schizophrenic, or there's nobody else there. I mean, you've got to have a rapping partner, right? So an alter ego has to be somehow produced. Well, the way you produce the alter ego is, of course, with mirrors. You always use mirrors for this; it's all done with mirrors. And we'll talk about that. Who is the reflection and who is the reality? Or whom. Actually it's not who you know, it's whom you know. And it's the same thing in . . . Who is the reality? Which one is the reality? Which one is not? Well, it depends. Which mirror are you looking at? Is the mirror the only reality, and the two reflections, and so forth?

Oh yes, the price that you pay for working with the pack of green is . . . working with the pack of green. In other words, the price you pay for teamwork, for team effort, is to be a member of the team, to be assimilated in that team, sucked in, assimilated, absorbed into it, and melding with it. And, when you look around, it's hard to meisnerize with folks that you just normally wouldn't even give the time of day to on the street. But here you are and you're learning to tolerate each other. Not just to tolerate each other, but to go beyond tolerating, to actually like each other. Is anyone there? And, to actually like each other, even love each other, appreciate each other, adore – I wouldn't go that far. No point.

So, now, in the Face of God, you have a tolerance level. It's kind of tough to be in the Face of God. And so the tolerance level is very, very unique to you, how much tolerance level there is. And I'll tell you a secret to that, a really, really fun secret. The secret to tolerance is to make the waking state *fun*.

But that's what it's like for me in the Absolute space. It's spotlights on you. There are two-thousand, three-thousand people out there, all talking . . . about me. You're thinking of the guys in the football game, the guys in the circle – and they're standing out there – they're talking about me. And they used to talk about my dad, Horace. He explained to me, 'cause I didn't know what they were doing in a huddle; they're talking about me.

The tolerance level is very interesting. I had a conversation with a doctor a while ago, an M.D. type, and we were talking about levels of pain and tolerance, and he said, "Yeah, if you're enjoying yourself, you're out there enjoying yourself, whatever it is you're doing, you're out there, you're playing soccer, or baseball, or basketball, or football – whatever it is. You're just having a great time. You get hurt. You hardly notice it. You *hardly* notice it. Because you're just not there at the moment. Later on, you'll deal with it." This was actually a part of a lecture, and I don't want to go into the whole thing about it, but we talked about the various aspects of pain.

One of the things that you might notice, for instance, a very obvious one, is in sex. Having a great time, you're having sex, and something happens. You get hurt. You just keep going. Because, jeez, you're having an orgasm. You don't want to stop in the middle of an orgasm. But also, if the phone rings, you're not going to get up and answer the phone. You just won't get up and answer the phone in the middle of an orgasm. It's just not the kind of thing you would do because your attention is rooted, so to speak. I wouldn't. But . . . that's me! But the reason you tolerate it is because of what we call love or lust, or both – love-lust, or lust for love, which is that you're busy obeying the organic directives, the procreative directives, just like imperatives, like the territorial imperative, the consumption imperative. All these imperatives, you see, and the procreation imperative is very, very powerful. Eating, sleeping and breeding – not in that order – are the imperatives that nature imposes upon you, because, otherwise, you would basically do none of those things . . . maybe.

You might sleep, but eating – why would you do that unless you felt you had to? And coupling – well, if you really examine it – I mean *really* examine what is going on there, and take away some of that personal relationship – the love aspect of it, you know, the fascination with it – you take that away, and it's just a job. You know, like commercial sex.

I've talked to thousands of hookers, because I was in a shop where they came to buy my essential oils, candles, incenses and herbs, and so on. So, to entertain your clients and to entertain themselves in-between clients, they left their cribs for a few minutes, went out to prowl around and get something to eat during the day, and they'd stop at my shop. And we'd talk, and they talked about how boring, how unutterably boring mechanical sex is. It's mechanical sex, it's just mechanical. It's just the mechanics of getting somebody off for money. And it's boring, boring, boring. But when you're with that perfect partner, it isn't boring at all, it's just so exciting. You'll do all kinds of things that you wouldn't normally do in order to satisfy that craving for, that lust for, love.

Now, if you can only apply that same thing to God, you'd have a hell of a lot more tolerance for God. You know what I'm saying? In the Face of God, love of God will keep it tolerable, much more so than if you're indifferent to God. But you've got to love God like a lover, 'cause that's what gets you through it. So, *agape* is a form of love that is not romantic, it's not sentimental, it's not personal. *Agape* – it's a very high love, but that high love can only be a love of God as a lover. In order to stand in the face, or be in the Face of God, be there as a lover . . . just a hint.

We'll talk later about gradations of the waking state and how you can actually increase your gradations along the waking state levels. We're going to play certain games which will help you with that. We'll also expose you to certain radiations. You need to learn to lust after the waking state rather than be repelled by it. Lust after it – actually *lust* after it. But also, you need to learn how to temper that lust for it – because you don't want to blast into the waking state on your own, alone, and take that whole burden by yourself. You want to have support and help in doing that, 'cause you don't want to take that *whole* pie; you want to take a *piece* of the pie. I'm telling you, you don't want the whole action.

Levels of tolerance are sometimes based on levels of frequency, how often something happens, and that has to do with cycles. There are a number of Trinity games, or Triad games. Trinity game – meaning one, two, three, infinity – is the basis, or the rule. I can explain this to you, but you first must understand that above all else, the pack of green rules. That's above everything else – the pack of green rules everything. No matter what you think might be important, the pack of green is more important than anything you could possibly think of.

There is a game which we used to play, which came to me through Sam Lewis, which is – and of course, Reshad Feild played this game as well: I – you – God – where you repeat: I, I, I, You, You, You, God, God, God. First of all, it's slightly incorrect. It's deliberately in the incorrect order. It should be: I – God – You, You – God – Me, and so forth. Godding is an action as well as an object, and a non-object, and so forth. God is actually more of an activity than a person, place or thing. So you think of God as a verb rather than as a noun, and you'll get closer to it. The I, I, I, You, You, You, God, God, God concept is based upon what is called the repetitions, and I'll explain that to you. This is where it's going to start departing from anything rational.

In a very high space, a very, very high-level space, a space which we'll call the waking state, things can occur in there. You could say something, do something, whatever it might be, which constitutes an element – we'll call it, an element – in the same way that a thing is maybe an element of an equation – an element. For instance, in words and word-making, you're going to string elements of the alphabet together to make words. If you say a word such as WoW, we're using WoW as an example of this because it's *World of Warcraft,* and we're experimenting with that. So we'll take the word W-o-W, WoW, and we'll just say that you say the word WoW three times in any given level of space. After that third repetition of the word WoW, the space must be broken if you're playing Trinity.

In a hardcore game of Trinity, any repetition of any kind three times constitutes a break in the space. You must, at that time, switch spaces in some way. Let's use words as an example of it, because it'll be good for you to understand it with words. So we'll use the word WoW. WoW is an element in itself. It's an exclamation, or a saying, or a speech, or a form of speech. And it is in itself complete, is it not? WoW . . . don't need anything else beyond that. And there's a lot of meaning implied there. WoW . . . WoW . . . WoW . . .

Wowww. There are lots of meanings implied there, in how it's said.

Provided that you're playing hardball, a real hardball game of Trinity, it isn't how you say it, it's that you said it. It isn't your intention whether you said it accidentally or deliberately. It's that you said it. Ah, um, ummm, ohh, gosh, gee, heck, hmm, hmm. And you're playing real hardball when you get hmm, hmm as . . . you get three hmms; hmms constitutes a break. When you encapsulate such a unit, an element, into a string of elements, it becomes part of an expression. When it becomes part of an expression, the expression itself is a module or a unit. Three repetitions of a single element in a string constitutes a break in the string. We'll get there as well. This is something you're going to have to work to understand, strive to understand how this works.

It's not something that comes to you immediately unless you're in the waking state, in which case, you know exactly what I'm talking about. So, in order to understand exactly what I'm talking about, I invite you to get into the waking state. Do this *now*. Good. Presumably, you're now all in the waking state, so you'll understand everything I'm talking about, which is good. We can consciously create using our own tolerances. You have to expand your tolerance beyond one, two, three, infinity. See, one WoW – that's a warning. Click – clicks in, uh-oh. I've done a WoW. I've said a WoW there. Oops, second WoW just happened. Oops, now the third WoW. Okay, break. That's it. Now we go back into the napping state. Okay, now we're in the waking state again. We'll try again. No repetitions three times, no repetitions three times, no repetitions – oh, I did it again. Almost did it again . . . almost . . . did it.

You can consciously expand that elemental structure, and here's how you do it. You take any given element that you can personally tolerate, any waking state that you can personally tolerate. In that waking state, you choose to ignore the repetitions of something. You choose to ignore the Trinity effect, and you just keep riding on your cheat, basically, is how you win. You're winning, not for yourself. So you cheat past the third repetition – WoW, WoW, WoW, WoW, WoW, WoW, WoW, WoW. And you turn it into a mantra loop. A mantra loop – actually, watch what happens. You have an element – WoW, another element – WoW, a third element, when said, breaks the loop. It breaks it! The third element breaks it. So clearly, that's not a cycle. You can continue the WoW-ing – WoW, WoW, WoW, WoW, WoW, WoW, WoW, WoW, WoW, WoW, WoW. It creates, at some point, past the third; it automatically goes to . . . it's one, two, three . . . and then infinity. The fourth WoW actually dedicates it to an infinity loop.

An infinity loop turns back on itself, klein bottle style, and forms what's called a waveform. That waveform is a non-linear wave. There are standing waves, sitting waves, lying down waves, dancing waves, running waves, jumping waves, waxing waves, briny waves. The structure of a waveform is determined by your decision as to where you're going to clip your reality structure. For instance, what you call peak. You're going to define peak. If you say WoW is the peak, it creates a certain waveform with WoW at the top. If you decide not to play the Trinity game, and to re-define peak, you can re-define the peak of a waveform, and thus change the structure of the waveform. You can see this on an oscilloscope – spiky waves, rolling waves, sine waves, all kinds of different waveforms –

but if you take it into a dimensional format, you actually can see mushroom-shaped waves, and so forth. You can start seeing them as, in their shapes, in their topological forms as well as their topographical forms. There's a topographical waveform. There's also a topological waveform, which may or may not be obviously connected to itself.

In order for tolerance to increase, let's say that you have a WoW factor where you're really very heavily socked into it – the waking state – and your tolerance for it is, basically, everything you're doing is just handling the waking state. That's all you're doing is handling the waking state. Everything's going toward that – I must handle the waking state. I've got to handle the waking state. You can use ESD loops – Erotic Spirit Dance loops – they were made for this purpose, to take some of the burden off you. Those ESD loops are someone's sacrifice. There is a sacrifice there allowing you to let go of some of the looping effect, and let that carry you. Let those carrier waves buoy you up, carry you up, boost you up, without you having to handle every single part of the waking state, all the various discomforts of the waking state. So it takes off some of the pain, some of the burden, some of the anguish of the waking state.

There's always a balance. There's always a balance game being played between energy and matter. In the waking state there is no matter. It doesn't matter. It's always energy. It's some form of energy, and that's all it is. There is no matter. It doesn't ever slow down below the speed of light, not ever; it's beyond photons. And it's a kind of energy which was called *shakti*, which is a wet energy. And that's not an oxymoron. There is such a thing as wet energy, and you need to look at that.

The price of help in the waking state . . . the price of help is that help arrives. And you have to learn to tolerate that instead of tolerating the thing you can't tolerate. So, in other words, there's a trade-off, there's a balance game between accepting help and getting help, or needing help and getting help. You have to really merge with that help. You have to let that help come, let that help be there. And that's hard because your box is constructed of your suffering. And your suffering box, the box you make for suffering is the box where you are alone, where you suffer alone. You suffer all your own anguish. You can identify that as lifetime anguish, lifetime suffering, and so forth. But it isn't. It really is much higher than that. It developed as an energy being. That's where your suffering first started, when you first started making boxes around yourself. Oh, by the way, the wet energy is also called *mana* as well as *shakti*.

We've covered the zone with the chimp-chump-champ zones. There's a game which we use – the Attentiacizer. This is a very good game for waking state, but I have an addition to that, which is "watch the clock," and as a group, I want you all to find a great clock. It will be used for this exercise. It should look like a train station clock and have a big, big sweep second hand. You can get huge antique-style clocks that are readable from thirty or forty feet away. It's got to be a big train station clock. You should all get together, chip in and send somebody as a representative to go find this for you. But I also have another one which we're going to work with that is called "Watch the Rock," and I'll explain that later. So, Watch the Rock is a very good exercise for you.

I would really like it to be a smooth action. You don't really want to have a tick-tick-tick, because that really doesn't tell you when you've lost it. It doesn't cut it fine enough. It needs to be a smooth action, which is why the attentiacizers are so unusual, because the tick movement is a usual movement for clocks these days. It's easier for them to tick them. Besides, it sells better.

You'll discover in the waking state that it's easier to tolerate infinity than it is to tolerate eternity. Eternity's a tough, tough nut. Infinity – no problem; can handle infinity until you start feeling the loops. When you start feeling yourself stretching out like a dachshund, or you start donuting out, or whatever it is that happens to you when you're in that state, you know, you could maybe feel a little uncomfortable from that. But, infinity is fairly easy to take. Eternity is very hard to take – which is not heaven or hell – but when is this going to end? So there are several important questions that Barbara and Adam asked in *Beetlejuice*.

Now POG rules. P-O-G R-U-L-Z – pog rulz. No matter what else happens, the pack of green is the necessity. The pack of green is what you keep together. The pack of green is what you keep in. That's what you're traveling with is the pack of green. That's what's important. If you can't give yourself to the pack of green, the pack of green will do you no good. It's useless to you. You've actually got to join it, be part of it, be responsible toward it and for it. Co-responsibility is really an important issue here.

The crown of creation is simply this; here's how it works: expansion and contraction both occur at the same time, if time is not understood to be a linear thing. At one and the same moment there's expansion and contraction. There's also: I eat you, you eat me. Something eats us. We eat something else. We eat and we're eaten. At the same time, we're eating and being eaten, if nothing else, by the action of oxygen. There's something eating you at all times, wearing you away at all times – physically, organically, at least, but also energetically; you're wasting away, you're dissipating. At the same time you're gathering. It's all coming in on you and it's all going out. You're expanding and contracting at one and the same time, and therefore, in that co-action, you get a phase-factor which is actually a waveform elimination process where one wave beats against another wave. All similar waves beat against each other. You have a reduction of your equation and you end up as you, which is what's left over after all the other waveforms have been subtracted out of you. So you're a unique waveform in the sense that you're the leftovers from whatever it is you started with.

We're working with virtual reality GODD levels. I'm starting to go back into the GODD editor, making levels. And many of you experienced the ultraviolet radiation from some of the slots that we worked with. We're doing the same thing out of the monitor screen. I'm hitting you with cleansing radiations out of there, and I'm trying to make games that are interesting for you to play so you'll actually be amused while the radiations are working on you rather than just sitting under a light, which is very boring. You can actually play *Capture the Flag* with some folks, and you're getting the radiations right off the screen. It covers everything. It's not just your face that gets the radiations, of course.

If you're having a problem with your conditioning, this lifetime conditioning, if you have any kind of lifetime, for instance, if you're a Catholic and you had your knuckles rapped by a ruler one too many times, and you basically succumbed to the Catholic conditioning, and you're always wrong, you're afraid of being wrong, you're afraid you'll burn in hell if you make a mistake, you know, the things you learn in Catholic school – you want to substitute something for that. You can't eliminate it, but you can actually substitute something. There's no way to eliminate a body of habits, but what you can do is substitute another body of habits for it. So pick one out of another lifetime that you had. As a Zen Monk perhaps – whatever it is – something with less conditioning perhaps, or maybe a little bit more amenable conditioning. And just put that in place. Just grab it from another lifetime. You're allowed to do that. You're entitled. If you don't know how to do that, it constitutes a workshop. Unity is created by separation, because separation produces yearning. That yearning acts upon you to create unity.

The POG shares responsibility for the waking state and increases the tolerance for the waking state, which is agreed to every single day. You have to re-agree every day. The waking state is always one day long, but a day can be defined very differently if you ignore minutes, you know, seconds, minutes, hours. That's not a day. A day is whatever it took to get from the beginning of the waking state to the end of the waking state. That's one day. The napping state also equals one day on the Darkside. Each one equals a day. So you have a day in the waking state and a day in the napping state. The napping state is your reward for having spent the day in the waking state. You get to nap for a day. That day is determined by you, based on where you clip your frequencies, where you clip your cycles. You have long cycles, short cycles, so a day could be twelve hours, twenty-four hours, whatever it might be. Or it could be three million years, whatever you choose, whatever your level of tolerance is – that's perfectly acceptable. Whatever your level of tolerance is for eternity, infinity and the other thing . . . that's fine. You get to do it that way.

When you're playing the Trinity game, if you need to extend your conscious state out a bit, you can use things like Erotic Spirit Dance loops or mantra loops to cheat past the automatic function, which will kill the waking state on the third repetition. It can be a repetition of a word, the blink of an eye, or just breathing. Three times breathing constitutes a triple, constitutes a trinity, constitutes, therefore, end of state. Like I said, a paranoid schizophrenic, a totally psychotic individual, would answer very well for the waking state. The waking state could be considered to be a state of ultimate, absolute psychosis. But that is the word. Don't forget the word "psychosis" comes to us from a man who couldn't keep his hands off his cigar or his daughter. Siggy Freud invented this concept. So, what he said was the waking state, basically, is nutty and the napping state is sane. If you believe that, then you have no chance whatever in the waking state. So you need to actually understand that what is called psychosis and paranoia – those are perfectly natural – are tools of consciousness. And they're used that way. They can be used artistically as Dali did.

What I was saying is that we'll get into a workshop situation and we'll explore this more. We'll have games to arouse the working state, to get you into the working state. Also, games that you can play in the working state to explore the working state. Also, kinds of work that you can do in the waking state, the working-waking state. The working-waking state is a state that is actually an applied waking state. So the waking state – working in it; the waking state – playing in it; the working state – staying in it. So those are the things that we'll explore. And getting into it – those are things that we'll have to explore in a workshop. It will have to be workshop application, where we actually do the exercises. We'll take some lab time; we'll then discuss a little theory.

Everything that we're going to be discussing and working with is going to be based on loops, cycles, frequency, wavelength and waveform. And so, in order to familiarize you with that, I'm going to have to have some help. I have some scientist friends here who are going to help me to make you understand what a waveform is, to make you understand what loops are, and what frequency, cycle and wavelength have to do with anything.

The waveform – what does it look like? What's the difference between one waveform, a complex waveform, and a simple waveform, for instance? What is beat frequency oscillation? How does it work? How is wave cancellation affecting you at all times? Always affecting you? How does it affect you? Why? How? And do you want to do anything about it? And if you do, do you need to? And if you need to, what do you do? So those are all areas of exploration.

I'm just giving you now what are called "highlights." And I notice that there are some things that I would call highlights, things that I consider very important, but those things we have to relegate to a workshop because we just can't put all those things into two hours. You just can't pack the work of many, many, many lifetimes into a two-hour package. It just can't be done. But this'll give you some heads-up anyway.

Yes, you'll find out what your defense mechanism against the working state is. You have a primary defense mechanism, a secondary defense mechanism, just as you have a primary profession, a secondary profession in the game of WoW. In *World of Warcraft*, you have a primary profession, secondary profession. You have a primary defense mechanism, and a secondary, and even tertiary (sometimes) defense mechanisms against the waking state. Those mechanisms – defense mechanisms – are called your box. That's the box that you built around yourself to keep yourself from the waking state, to keep yourself where you are comfortably napping. It's your comfort zone. You build a comfort zone around yourself in the form of a box. Getting that box down is going to be most of your struggle.

Also, repetitions don't cause a loop or a cycle until the third repetition. Two repetitions don't constitute – even the third repetition itself does not constitute – a cycle. It's a triangle. But as soon as you infinitize the repetitions, going to four repetitions or more, you've created a loop which has created a cycle. A cycle means simply having to do with frequency. It happens again and again and again and again. It happens many times. How often it does happen constitutes the frequency; how much it happens constitutes the amplitude, in what way it does happen constitutes the simplicity or complexity of the waveform, which is generated from that particular loop.

Loops tend to loop back on themselves. Now, you can decide how you can create a loop – mantra loops in particular – but you can create any kind of loop: an action loop, a thought loop, a loop composed of emotion, a loop composed of expression of various kinds, artistic expression, business loops – anything you want to create; you can create a loop to your level of tolerance. That is a way of taking burden, but you have to do it consciously. It's not just getting into a loop and marching forward. That's not a loop. That's not the same thing. And you can decide how to determine the loop, how to make the loop of the elements that you're going to use.

You'll use, let's say, one element – the WoW factor. So we'll use the WoW factor as one. We want to instead match frequencies, or we want to offset frequencies. We want to start factoring the phasing which is a form of filtering. When you use subtractive frequencies to create a third left-over frequency, the two frequencies are the two things that don't match. Wet energy doesn't match; it's an oxymoron. When you mix the two things, you get a third thing which is *nit ahin, nit aher*, which is Latin for neither here nor there, which is to say, a third force.

That third force is actually the force which results. It's the resultant force, which is neither energy nor matter. It's neither dry nor wet. It's *nit ahin, nit aher*. It's not this, it's not that. It's something else. It's leftover from two things that don't normally merge, that cannot merge.

So you would create a filter through which you would cheat repetitions beyond the third repetition. You decide, "All right, we'll not cut our space. We're not going to cut the waking state if we trinitize. We're going to just go blasting on ahead without the trinity factor." You have to choose some filter, and choosing a filter at that point . . . phase factors. It factors the phasing effect. Factoring means the same thing, by the way, as it does in bookkeeping. In accounting, you're going to factor something. Factoring is actually a mathematical action, let's call it. But it also is a direct action of consciousness upon itself, and not the space, because at this point, you can't even call it a space. Consciousness without an object is also consciousness without space, without a universe, because a universe is an object. Pure consciousness is itself an object.

So the waking state is the true remembrance of the Self, the I as God, as God the Absolute, which is beyond description, beyond Godness, beyond Absoluteness – tag, you're it. When you've been tagged, you accept the tag – you have to tag yourself – you tag yourself as It. All right, and when you do that, you assume responsibility for Godness. I said it before, but I wanted to make sure that you understood that clearly.

When you take an infinity loop of something – let's say it's crocheting – you can tolerate crocheting, so you accept that repetition that you're going to get into of crocheting or weaving, shuttle back and forth, or spinning or turning a pot, whatever it might be – or doing the books, or schlepping around some sales cases, or going door-to-door with magazines, whatever it is – that you accept this loop, this infinity loop, which is basically your personal ability to share whatever burden you can share. Now there might be several loops going on. There might be several infinity loops, but let's just address one such loop. And so, the composite of all those loops that you accept – all the infinity loops that you're running, as your part of Godness – is fulfilling your level of responsibility for Godness. All those loops that you're running past the trinity, past the three-point, the composite, is called your "karma." In other words, your responsibility that you've taken on yourself – that's your karma. It also is your life. It's

what you experience, it's what you do, it's what happens to you
. . . and so forth.

What typically happens to you, that's your karma, that's your
life, those are your loops, those are your cycles. And you go
through them again, and again, and again, and again, and again
– the same thing over and over and over and over – that's your
karma. So karma is actually a wheel; it's called a wheel of
karma. Those are all created by loops which you've taken upon
yourself. But mostly, you've taken the loops that create a
comfort zone for yourself, a napping zone. So you have a
napping karma which is what we call an automatic karma
rather than conscious karma.

When you accept responsibility for Godness in a variety of
ways . . . I'm going to show you how to do that, not just
describe it. Yet, you can, deliberately and directly, show how
you can create those responsibility loops, conscious loops.
When you do that, you're going to be transforming your life
from automatic karma to conscious karma. And you can do
that with a variety of different kinds of repetitions, of course.
They're a mantra . . . repetitions. But there are many other
kinds. There are work repetitions of all kinds.

Everything constitutes repetition. The whole thing in
accepting responsibility in this method is accepting the fact
that something's going to happen over and over and over and
over again . . . and many such things. You're actually going to
have a whole plethora, a whole grouping, a bunch. You'll be
grabbing hold of the fasces, the bundle of arrows, which
represents your acceptance of these responsibility loops. And I
know that that's kind of vague at this point, but we're going to
get it very specific and actually lab-test it right in front of you.

Here's a cheat that you might work on, which is called the Changement Technique. And that is where you never repeat anything ever more than once. You just do something, and then you never repeat it ever again. What happens is if you try to avoid trinitizing by changement, you'll end up obsessive/compulsive . . . you don't want that. Obsessive/compulsive – "Oh, I can't walk around the chair the same way twice . . . oh, three times . . . oh, I've really done it to myself!" – and so on. So those variations on theme: what happens is as soon as you start varying something, you start repeating the variations. And then the variation itself becomes eventually trinitized, and the space drops, gets killed.

Here's a way of saying it: lengthening an element by the process of ever-changement – weaving it into a much larger expression in which the expression itself does not contain more than two repetitions of any single defined or definable element – leads to a place in which the avoidance itself becomes an infinity loop, which is called automatic karma.

Also, we do not exercise choice in the pack of green – nobody does. Packs of green (POGs) always have a team leader and two fire team leaders. But those are changeable, depending upon areas of expertise. And so we allow ourselves to be used in a particular way and to avail ourselves of the knowledge and, perhaps, the wisdom that we're exposed to, and also, of course, to any radiation cleansing that obtains from that.

I wanted to mention to you, by the way, that the Bardo maps that I produce are color-coded to the tarot. The particular tarot that I'm color-coding to is the Pamela Coleman-Smith tarot deck that was re-issued by a kid who did this wonderful deck. It's just finally come back out on the market again. The Frankie Albano deck, that's closest. I had a deck of Pamela Coleman Smith. It's so rare; there are maybe four or five copies of it existing anywhere. The Albano is a very, very close match to the Pamela Coleman-Smith, and you can get it for thousands of dollars less. It's very cheap. It's Stuart Kaplan that produced this deck.

The Bardo is color-coded. Areas of danger are going to be red. Areas of some danger are going to be orange. Areas of extreme humanity will be in the yellow coding. Those are the chimp zone areas. So if you see red brick all around you, you're going to be in the Brute World or the Hell World, somewhere in that range, and so forth. It's also color-coded, it's Qabbalistically coded and tarot coded. Of course, the tarot is nothing more than a shorthand version of the Qabbalah. The 21 paths are delineated in a particular way, the spheres are delineated, and so forth. That's all – the spheres and the paths. And you know that the Qabbalah – the Sepher Sephiroth – is a three-dimensional, not a two-dimensional item. It's drawn in medieval version of what a double-stacked cube is. It's a stacked cube, a double cube.

What happens to the pack of green in the waking state is pretty much what happens in ladies' luncheons. Everyone serves as a host or hostess once a week. So you'll maintain, and we'll come to your universe. "Okay, whose turn is it now to maintain?" So, you're hosting actually. Everyone gets a chance to be a hostess. You have to be a hostess because you're the Queen of Space, the infinite procreator, the great fountain of wisdom. I forget the other ninety-three. In fact, you can become, at some point, if you are a very good Queen of

Space, the King of Queens. But then, of course, you can cap that by becoming the Queen of Kings, and so forth. It goes in and out, up and down, back and forth.

I'll take some questions because questions will undoubtedly lead to further clarification of this already very complex and almost un-understandable subject.

However, let's say the very basis is that nobody tags you, you tag yourself "it" when you assume the waking state. You take responsibility for your own tag. Tag, you're it. Tag, I'm it. However that happens, nobody tagged you, nobody's going to tag you, nobody's going to shock you with it or shoot you full of it. You're not going to go to Guru G and have him touch you; it's garbage because somebody else's taking responsibility for you being in the waking state. Ultimate form of paranoia; ultimate form of hypnosis at the same time. How can that be?

Somebody else takes responsibility to send you into the waking state. No, that's not the waking state. It's actually a deeper form of hypnosis. A bigger box? No, a smaller box, a tighter box, in which somebody is directing you to the waking state. It's not the waking state you're going to. It's a deep state of napping in which you feel good. Why shouldn't you feel good? Because you're not responsible.

Anyway, any questions about this? You have a chance now to throw your questions out here. I may or may not be able to answer them.

Neville: Can you talk about cheating past that trinity? What is it . . . oscillating in and out?

Yes, of course I can. If you say the word WoW three times, you're out. So you set up a bunch of chairs, and everyone starts talking in tongues. If you should happen, during the course of that, to utter the word WoW, or anything three times, you're out. It's like musical chairs.

It's a counting-out form of game. We can actually play that by everybody starting to just talk. Just say things, not whatever's on your mind, just automatic talking. If you begin doing that, you'll discover that at some point you'll repeat yourself, and then you'll go, "Ooh, I mustn't think of the word hippopotamus again. No elephant, no WoW; don't say WoW, don't say WoW, don't say WoW. Oh, I said it! Oh, damn, I can't believe I said WoW a second time. That's so ridiculous. I've been trying not to say WoW. Oh no! I just did it. I'm out." So, you sit down, you're gone, you're asleep, you're napping now. You're in the napping state. So we'll be playing games like that so that we'll illustrate what happens in those things.

Iven: Just change the rules?

Yes, you change the rules, exactly. It's called no clip.

Iven: What if you change the rules three times?

Well, it depends. That's where the filtration happens. You decide what constitutes outness. That'll change the waveform. That changes the waveform because it changes the frequency. It changes the frequency; the amplitude changes everything. So, you're going to cut it – the peak is the top of any cycle. Any cycle has a peak. It also has a trough. You're going to clip that peak wherever you say, however you say – slightly askew, fine. It creates a different waveform as well as a different level of amplitude. You're going to clip it. You're going to decide that the trinity game is off today. We're not playing the trinity game. So you'll be spending a day in your life. A day in *the* life? No, a day in *your* life. Then when you stop clipping, and you let the trinity game happen, and you endure that, you will experience a day in *the* life as opposed to *your* life. There's a difference.

Where you clip it makes the difference. Actually, learning how to clip it, learning how to cheat – cheats and codes are really where it's at. And you're not cheating for yourself, you're cheating for the greater good. You're accepting responsibility, taking some load, some of the weight. You know . . . like when you pull into Nazareth, and you ask somebody to take a little load off. In the '60s, that's all we sang about. "The waking state, the waking state, I'm going to wash that brain right out of my skull." We all try to achieve, we all try to get into San Jose, and we all wanted to know the way. But the way to San Jose is not "the way."

A tree is a tree and a mountain is a mountain and a rock is a rock, but they also aren't. So we're exploring the aren't, the not tree, the not rock, the not mountain. And that's an end of existence which normally you don't explore, normally you don't go there. So we will go there. We'll enter into levels of fear and paranoia. Fear, anger, frustration, loneliness, jealousy, envy and pride – these are all defense mechanisms. They're defense mechanisms against the waking state. It's what you do to prevent yourself from being in the waking state. Business – "I'm really busy right now. I would love to be in the waking state, but I'm really busy right now. Can you come back later?"

"I hate the Empire as much as anybody, but I just can't do it right now. I'm needed out there in the fields. I've gotta go out there and program the robots and the droids. I just can't, I can't, I can't go after the Empire right now. Certainly not the Emperor, not directly. You know, learn to be a Jedi warrior." Who has the time for this? Well, actually nobody does. That's, of course, the point. Nobody has the time to dedicate to this stuff, or the energy to dedicate to it – the time, the energy, the space to dedicate – everything. But you've got to throw it all in there.

You really have to dedicate yourself to this in a way that makes an obsessive/compulsive look absolutely normal. So obsessive/compulsives would be pitying you at some point. OCDs will all gather around and say, "Ohhhh. Jesus, what a shame, look at this. That's just awful, what you're doing to yourself; it's just terrible." Yes, isn't it terrible? It is a deliberate step into the state of paranoia, the state of fear, the state of anxiety. All these things will just pummel you. They'll just come crashing in on you when you enter the waking state because you're opening those doors all up. That's Pandora's Box.

The Pandora's Box doesn't have any sides or top or bottom to it. It's all open. There's no box. Pandora's Box is a boxless box, the box that expands to the limits of the universe – the big box. Then you take that down. And now you're at raw frontage. You're at the very front – the crown of creation. There you are.

What are you going to do in that kind of condition? What are you going to do in that space? You've got to get into it before you can find out what you're going to do there. "Let's see, what will I do, what will we do when we get to Disneyland? Oh man, we're going to do such and such, blah, blah, blah." Well, you can speculate all you want, but what if Disneyland is closed or Wallyworld is closed the day you get there? What are you going to do, take a BB gun and hold it to the guard and say, "Take me on the rollercoaster"? Yes, some people do. Is that clear? Is that a good answer for you? It's where you clip it that makes the difference. The cheats and codes are . . . give me twenty hours with you to show you the cheats and codes in lab, where you're actually dealing with the waking state, and you're trying to handle it. Here are the cheats and codes that help you handle it.

Okay, any other questions? I want to hear some more questions. Yes, I saw one back there somewhere.

M.A.: You mentioned about hypnosis . . . .

Hypnosis is defined in my usage of it, not stage hypnosis. Hypnosis is the giving away of responsibility, whether deliberately or not – the giving away of responsibility for oneself.

M.A.: Okay, and I was thinking along those same lines about lack of will, a lack of true will.

Well, nobody has true will. You've got to borrow will. You have to borrow it from somewhere. What you do is you attach yourself to a star, hook yourself to a star, and use the greater will to boost your own. That's a real simple solution to it. It works really great. Just find something bigger and hook onto that and use that will. And if you can find something bigger, hook onto that, so you've got a greater and greater will. You don't try to use your own will because your own will is pitiful! So you need to find a will that's much greater than yours, which would be better. And that will just hoist you right up. See, you can't hoist yourself up by your own bootstraps.

MA: And you can use that to get in the waking state as well?

Yes, you can use it for just about anything. But then it's

balanced by necessity, and the responsibility also has to do with compassion and considerateness and kindness and courtesy. These are things that actually are part of our learning to work together, learning to work in these areas. When you borrow higher will, you're also borrowing the responsibility level, so your niceness factor goes up. The more will you have, the nicer you're going to be, the less fearful you're going to be, and the less angry with yourself for being afraid you're going to be.

Anger is just a result of being afraid of something, so you get angry. That's all anger ever is is just you're pissed off that you're afraid, so you lash out and you try to put it outside yourself. The cause of your fear and anger – you try to make it go outside yourself somewhere. So you don't take responsibility for that.

Kelly: You also once told me that it's also humiliation. You feel humiliation over feeling fear.

Oh, of course. Oh you're so pissed off at yourself for feeling fear – oh my God! Oh, absolutely. "So, I'm really pissed off at myself – not at me; I'm pissed off at you because you made me afraid. That's what it is; yes, you – whoever it is."

Iven: It works.

If it hadn't worked so well, you wouldn't be here. That's one area that we're going to be dealing with in the workshop and we're going to have to have a couple of days at least. Other questions? Wow, a lot of questions – all right. Just said WoW. Well, that's it! You never know. But that's how it happens. Oh, that's it, you see? Oh, I said WoW. No, no, no, okay so I said WoW. Go ahead. That's the cheat. That's the cheat right there.

xliv

David: That's the cheat. We accept the cheat. Can you say more about responsibility loops?

You're going to take a bite of eternity and infinity and that other thing, some bite of that. And you're going to turn it into something that you take on yourself. It's a burden you take on yourself – some part of the waking state for which you're accepting responsibility, and to the level that you can accept it right now. So you would create through cheats. You have to ignore the fact that the trinities are happening. And so you accept certain trinities and you infinitize those. It's very specific, and it's very specific to you. And we will all have a different way of doing this.

David: Exactly, it just feels like there's a very personal . . .

It's uniquely personal, but at the same time, it's very universal. It's actually a personal universality. Or a universal persona. Well, it's the universal . . . it's the personal constant with the universal chaos. Look, with a totally chaotic universe, the consciousness that's appropriate to total chaos is a totally chaotic consciousness. Tolerance for that from an ordered consciousness is very hard. It's hard to actually go from an ordered consciousness to a chaotic consciousness all at once. So we're going to take little bites of it at a time.

Get used to eating this stuff. It's like resident food in *Defending Your Life*. It tastes really bad, you know. Well, you get used to it. Like arugula – if you can get used to arugula, you can get used to anything. You're eating crunchy gym socks – very, very used gym socks. Mind if I ask you a question? Would you wash out a pair of socks for me? What a surprise, Captain Spaulding. It might be a surprise to you. It's been on my mind for weeks (reference to a Marx Brothers movie).

That's arugula. If you can get used to arugula, you can get used to anything, absolutely anything, and consciousness is well within your grasp. It's true.

Okay, there was another question over here.

Kelly: Can I say something to that? At the same time, from order to chaos, it's difficult. We experience anguish, but the other way around works too. Right? Where the chaos becoming order . . .

It's like stuffing yourself into a tiny little box.

David: It may be just as painful.

That actually is part of what you do in your sacrificial structure. In your sacrificial act, you will, of course, accept a box which will be your part of Godness – your share – whatever share you can take of that, for as long as you can take it. And then, you might not be able to for awhile – go, waah, I can't, I gotta let it go, whoa ho, I can't wuh huaa . . . take it somebody. And somebody will take it. And you'll say, "I'll take it later. Not now, later, okay? Later." And it can't always be *not now*. It has to be at some point.

"Okay, I'm ready. All right, I'll do it. Okay, give it to me. Oh, oh, no, uuck, here it comes again. Whuaah. I've got it. Okay. Oh, somebody take it. Quick. I can't do it anymore . . ." and so forth. It's just how much you can take, when you can take it; it's all different, it's all variable. That's your karma, that's your level of acceptance, your level of responsibility, of acceptance for responsibility for Godness. . . your chunk, your share of the pie. You get your share of the pie.

When you are in the highest level of consciousness, you don't want to eat, do you? No! You wouldn't want to eat. You don't want to eat, you don't want to have sex, you don't want to go to the bathroom – no body functions, nothing. If somebody hands you a bowl of oatmeal and says you've got to eat one bite and chew it, knowing what it is, and swallow it, knowing what it is, and feel it going down, knowing what's happening – you've got to do that. All awake, all the waking state, you've got to have a spoonful of oatmeal. That would be a conscious loop that you took on yourself. Nobody wants to eat the oatmeal. Believe it.

Carlos: I was just wondering . . . so how can I access that state?

We're going to do a workshop, and in that workshop I'm going to present laboratory techniques, lab techniques for you to actually enter the waking state right then and there, smack dab right then and there. You're going to do it; you're going to do it right there in front of everybody, in front of God and everybody. Access the waking state – not just access it, but be in it. And whatever happens in that waking state, you agree to handle.

Carlos: And then once in there, we can begin to find out what we can do there?

Look, here's an example of something. Do you have a job?

Carlos: Yes.

What kind of job?

Carlos: I drive a school bus.

You drive a school bus. Before you drove a school bus, did you actually know what it was going to be like?

Carlos: No.

No. Couldn't possibly. Okay. Let's see . . . Bill, you've got a job, right?

Bill: Yes.

What do you do?

Bill: I do produce at Briarpatch.

You do?

Bill: I put out produce.

You put out produce at Briarpatch.

Bill: Yes.

Was there a time before that when you didn't do that job?

Bill: Yes.

When you had never done that job or anything like it?

Bill: True.

Did you know what you'd be able to do within that job until you got there?

Bill: No.

Okay, you're discovering even now things that are available to you that you didn't know were available. Driving a bus, you can do things, but you have to be driving a bus in order to understand what you can do with that situation. In the waking state, unless you're in it, actually in it, immersed in it, totally immersed in it, total immersion – they duck you down once, they duck you down a second time, a third time . . . come to think of it, that's the last thing I remember. So, full immersion – only then can you really, really, really know what it's like, what's available to you, what you can do there.

You can't do that until you're actually in the space. And there's no amount of explanation that's going to help you because all you're going to do is just cool yourself out. Okay, what's it going to be like? Well, it will be . . . and then you're asking a question that really is unanswerable unless you're actually there.

How will it be, this end of which I've spoken, Brother Emory? It will be as . . . there'll be a mighty rending of the skies and (mumbles, in an English accent) the valley shall rise and the mountains shall fall and great shall be the tumult thereof, I should think. Will the veil in the temple be rent asunder? Yes, the veil in temple is always rather dodgy. Will there be a mighty wind then? Yes, there'll be a mighty wind if the word of God is anything to go by. (In a deep, raspy voice) Will this wind be so mighty as to lay low the mountains of the earth? Whaaat? And so forth (a skit from Beyond the Fringe).

They are all questions that are designed to cool you out and, actually, to keep you napping on the way to the waking state, until you get to the waking state itself. And you say, "Here we are at Disneyland. Who's got E-tickets? Nobody? Did anybody think to get the coupon books, the free coupon books that the airlines give out? No? Okay, so we'll have to pay for our admission here. Let's pay for it. Everybody get a book . . . *everybody* get a book. How many E-tickets you got in the book? What . . . three? And fifty A-tickets, twenty-five B-tickets. What're you going to do? Hang on the carousel? For what? Fifty times? Come on! You're going to throw away, give away the As, the Bs, the Cs. All you want are the Ds and the Es. You want to go on the what?

David: The Matterhorn.

The Matterhorn (referring to the play, *Creation Story Verbatim*, also by E.J.). Yes, you want to go on the Peter Pan ride? You want to go on the Haunted Mansion? And, of course, you want to eat at all those great restaurants that Disneyland has. Oh man, you can put your tuna sandwich right out there on the table and sit right on the table while you eat it, like everybody else does. You don't really know what it's going to be like till you get there. So, what I'm proposing is let's get there, let's be in the waking state together, and let's explore what that's like and see what we can do there. What can happen there? Just got time for maybe one or two more questions.

Kelly: You spoke about the Great Work being a network of beings that have basically assumed responsibility for . . . .

Co-responsibility, each to their own measure, each group and each individual to their own unique measure. In other words, you're never asked to do more than you can do. Never.

Kelly: Okay. Now, is it safe to say borrowing from a will that is bigger than my own?

Higher.

Kelly: Higher than my own. Am I tapping into this network in doing so?

No, you need to apply the will. You can't just tap into the will. It has to be applied will. And the action is very specific. The action of taking consciousness, accepting the waking state, is a very active form of work and play. And in order to do it, you really must consciously do this. You can't stumble into the waking state and call it work. And, the waking state doesn't last very long. It trinities out really quickly and you have to re-establish it. It trinities out really fast.

You'll hit a repetition, and a second, and a third repetition, and wham! It's gone! You've got to re-establish it and do it

l

again, set up the standing wave again. The wave breaks eventually. It breaks. It breaks under pressure from within, not from outside. It's always internal pressure that breaks the wave.

Let's leave that there. That's a good question, and I want you to bring that up when we do a major workshop in this.

Kelly: Oh, believe me, I'll bring it up, and more.

You will. You'll bring up more than that, as a matter of fact, star barf not withstanding. One of the things you're going to learn to do is turn yourself inside-out; you'll learn to handle star barf; you'll learn how to deal with emanations of energy and intrusions of energy – all that kind of thing. That's all part of the waking state. That's all part of the stuff that's normal and natural in the waking state. Those are the issues in the waking state. The issues that you have in the napping state don't apply in the waking state, not at all. They're just not relevant, not at all relevant. So you'll be looking at issues like, "How do I breathe?" You guys all have the air. Can you breathe out a little bit? Come on, I need a little bit. Come on (folks breathing out).

Not like that! Come on! No noob breathing . . . just breathe. Thank you. Okay, you didn't notice, but for at least a minute you weren't breathing. Did you notice that now, looking back at it? You weren't breathing at all. Now you're breathing, you see. In the waking state, that becomes very significant. It's an issue, right? You wouldn't normally think of it in the biological state. You'd say, "Well, I'm not breathing for the moment, you know (breathing in) . . . Now I am . . . (breathing out)." Oh, because biological imperatives are different from consciousness imperatives – totally different. It's a different world.

You'll live in a different world, a world of the paranoid, a world of the schizophrenic, a world of the openly and rabidly psychotic. I suggest that when you do this, you at least put on a tie! At least put on a tie. What I mean by that is tie on the bed, rope out the window. That's not a pick, it's a pig. A pig is a hog. You know what a hog is? . . . Not that kind of . . . (reference to a Marx Brothers movie)

There are different issues. As you achieve the waking state, it will be very evident because your issues will change. You get what I'm saying? Your issues – they'll be less personal and more universal. At the same time, they'll be more personal in the higher sense. You'll have issues – like issues about breathing, issues about not enough ultraviolet radiation in here . . . there's just not enough. That becomes an issue.

There are many issues that are not tolerable to you in the waking state and, therefore, it keeps you from the waking state. So those issues need to be resolved. And your biological issues, if they are imperative in you, if they are burying you, if you're buried under a heap of biological issues – you first have to clear the overburden of biological issues before you can even begin to start looking for alchemical stuff. You'll find that there'll be mining, refining, and of course, ultimately, some whining. That whining is about issues that you have never addressed because they're beyond organic, beyond biological issues.

When I am in the waking state, I have a lot of sensation, but I don't have a body. How can I explain this to myself? Well, it's like asking a doctor, "You know, doctor, it hurts when I go like this." And the doctor's got to say, "Don't go like that.

Don't keep tickling it. Don't keep exploring that. If it hurts, then don't do that." All these biological imperatives are crashing in on me. I'm upset, I'm angry, I'm jealous, I'm envious, I'm this, I'm that, and so on. And someone's getting more than me, and I'm getting all the burden and it's all happening to me. And I 've got to cook and clean and . . . yadda, yadda, yadda. So, the yadda, yadda, yadda principle . . . see, there's a repetition of three right there. And the way to convert that is by deliberately clipping that, and saying yadda, yadda, yadda, yadda, yadda, yadda, yadda, yadda, yadda, yadda, yadda, yadda, yadda, yadda, yadda, yadda, yadda, yadda, yadda, yadda . . . and really get into it . . . yadda, yadda, yadda, yadda, you know. There's a way, and what you're doing is you're rolling over the tag, you're out. And you say, "No, I'm not out. I don't need no stinkin' badge (movie reference). I'm going to keep going. WoW, WoW, WoW,WoW, WoW, WoW, WoW, WoW, WoW, WoW, WoW, WoW, WoW, WoW, WoW, WoW, WoW . . . try and stop me. WoW, WoW, WoW, WoW, WoW."

You actually begin to say, "I'm starting to enjoy it. WoW, WoW, WoW . . ." At first you weren't, but now you're kind of liking it. Eventually you will get your tolerance up for things that you didn't have tolerance for. The pack of green is the very first unit of tolerance you need to handle. You need to handle the pack of green, accepting the pack of green, being part of the pack of green, and liking it, actually enjoying being part of this pack of green, *this* pack of green, not just *any* pack of green, not just an *imaginary* pack of green, not a pack of green that you're theorizing you might some day be a member of, no, this pack of green right now, guys. This is it. This is the pack of green, see?

So that is an area that we need to explore practically; you can't just explore it theoretically. You can't just say, "Well, if I were in the waking state, I'd . . ." No, no, no. You're in the waking state, now what are you going to do with it, wise guy? You wanted it; now you're in it. Okay, now what?" Basically, what I'm doing is calling your bluff. You say you want the waking state, fine. Let's call your bluff, and let's get into the waking state together and see what you do with it. I'd be curious to see what you do with it. Wouldn't you? So let's find out. That'll be good. We can find out right now, and we can keep finding out, and we're going to do that.

Okay, one more question I have available. Yeah, go ahead, Patty.

Pat: You used the phrase "lust for the waking state."

Yeah, lust for the waking state and lust for love.

Pat: Could you say just a little bit more about that?

It's an extreme yearning without desire, the way we use it. The way you use it biologically is it's extreme desire without yearning.

Pat: And so what would you use as the stimulus to create that yearning?

Well, it wouldn't be a boyfriend or a girlfriend.

Pat: Correct. It's not gonna be an object.

Oh no. It could be, but it's not a boyfriend or a girlfriend. To create a lust for the waking state, you have to take your present lusts, your biological lusts, away. You have to clear the overburden. And the way to do that is one by one you substitute a waking state lust for a biological lust. It's a slow process. It takes awhile.

Pat: Substitution rather than elimination?

You can't eliminate. You can never eliminate. All you can do is substitute. There's no way of eliminating any habits, but you can substitute habit for habit.

Pat: So we're back to the question of the Beloved.

What about it? . . . the Beloved. What about the Beloved?

Pat: That's what that is.

All right, you got the Beloved right there in front of you. Now what are you going to do? See, that's calling the bluff right there. Okay, let's see you do something about it. Go ahead.

Kelly: It seems to me that you can. My experience with yearning has been that there was something bigger than me that yearned *through* me.

No, no, no, no, no, it's *you* yearning, and it hurts. You want that, whatever it is. You want that. Okay? And it doesn't have to be an object.

Kelly: It leads to annihilation, though, correct? Yearning?

Yearning, no, because if it does . . . .

Kelly: Then it is a different experience.

No, no, it's got to be permanent yearning. It has to be a permanent separation. That's the whole concept of *Ha Satan*. The Holy Adversary is: God splits off a portion of God into the Holy Adversary, which is the other side of the mirror. Oh, by the way, you'll notice in the GODD Levels now that many of the signs are backwards. This is because you're in Mirrorland. You're actually *derrière le miroir* – you're behind the mirror. So you're seeing the mirror images. We've had all the signs. I made them all so they're backwards now. So you have to read them backwards. So, Gemini is Inimeg.

Kelly: I'm referring to an experience I had that I told you about in which I was annihilated over and I wanted to throw myself into the fire to be annihilated even more . . . .

Okay, that's the moth effect.

Kelly: But there was yearning behind that. And when that experience happened . . . clearly, it wasn't this character that you see here.

Yes, but you see the annihilation itself, if you're being annihilated, then you were un-annihilated as well. In-between the annihilations, you set up a process, or a cycle, of annihilation.

Kelly: It was . . . it was cycles, it was . . . .

Well then, it can never be permanent to work, to truly work; the annihilation can't be permanent. It has to be temporary. So, in other words, you can create lust by taste, and then by separation, by tasting it, and then separation, tasting and separating, tasting and separating, tasting . . . You can have this great one of these Boston crème pies – have a taste of it. Ahhhh. Ten years from now you can have another taste of it. See, whatever it might be. Whatever it is you really want to have, or really want to get into, really want, whatever it is, pull it away from yourself. But the waking state is not what you are yearning for. You don't lust for the waking state itself.

You don't lust actually for the waking state. You're going after it in a very, let's say, clinical way. But now, for instance, the highest form of love, *Agape´*, is not clinical, it's not removed, it's not dissociated; it's very involved, it's very, very, sensitive and very feeling. But it isn't romantic, it isn't sentimental, it isn't biological. And it's not expressed that way.

One more.

Neville: I was hoping that . . . you say that you can't change them, but I thought these radiations could erase them, or maybe mitigate them, or somehow transform them. I was hoping that . . . .

You can dissolve something to the degree that you're able to work on it. You get the overburden off and then you're expected to do something, otherwise, the overburden will come right back.

If you don't brush your teeth constantly, the plaque will come back. You can go in and get help from the dentist, which is the cleansing radiations. Go ahead and get help, and they take off the plaque, they take off the . . . you know . . . all the crud that's been gathering on your teeth. Even though you've been doing really good, you've been brushing your teeth every day, just like you're supposed to. You brush your teeth, you floss, you stick the little thing in there and you get the little brush in there and you floss the thing. And you're using the electric, the sonic care, and you're getting your teeth all clean. Every couple of months, three months, four months, you go in, you get your teeth cleaned, and you still have some crud on there. If you just let that crud accumulate on there, you're going to go in there and just get the cleanings, then you're really not doing anything about your dental care. You're not doing right.

Expecting somebody else to clean your teeth for you . . . that's the cleansing radiation. The cleansing radiation gets 'em down, but they're going to crud up no matter how much care you take. They're going to crud back up again and you're going to need more cleansing radiation. And you take it down, and you're going to work on it some more. Keeping your teeth clean is a hard job, it's an applied job.

Keeping yourself clean and clarified in the waking state is a job that requires repetitive work. You need to go out to actually enter into a cleansing – a full cleansing. And *that* I recommend every four months, a full cleansing. Three months, four months, a full cleansing; three months is better. So every three months you have a cleansing which we can arrange for in the form of a workshop, if you like. Have a cleansing which is equivalent to the cleansing that you'd have on your teeth, but then your responsibility is to keep it as clean as you can until the next cleansing. And don't depend on that cleansing to take care of the stuff that you haven't handled. In other words, you should try to keep it so that you don't need to have any care, or any minimal care, at that cleansing point.

When you're doing repetitive cleansing, it really is like brushing your teeth, which is . . . first of all, we're introducing you to cleansing through the use of *Diablo 2*. That is not really cleansing radiation. It's not going to do it for you. All it's going to do is teach you how to use the mouse and keyboard, actually, to some degree, get you some computer skills. Then you're going to go through some other areas like WoW and Team Fortress, and so on, which will get your skills up a little more. Then you'll be qualified to go into the GODD levels which requires such a level of expertise with the mouse and the keyboard that you're going to think, "My God, why didn't they train me for this?" Well, we did, but the training is nowhere near the actuality.

The actuality of working in the GODD levels is so far beyond what you think it's going to be, and yet, that's where we can deliver, not only the cleansing radiations, but also teaching games. There are also games in there. And that will put you into the waking state. We're going to get into that and show you how you can use the gaming to get into the waking state itself. That is a nifty procedure – to use the games to actually *activate* . . . I shouldn't say access. I don't like the word access – to *activate* the waking state in yourself. Then you use a higher will. There you use a borrowed will, there you use borrowed technique, there you use borrowed gaming. The game, in this case, is a kind of game like you'd play a game to teach somebody how to sew, or how to knit, or something like that, or how to play a piano; you play a certain game to do this.

Now, Doc, you've recently gotten into the GODD levels. Do you see what I'm talking about? Now that you've gotten into the GODD levels and tried to work them, do you understand what I'm talking about, the mechanism about the amount of control you have to have in order to work in this? It's incredible. It's far more than you're actually prepared for even when you're finished with all the other stuff. You're still not going to be ready for the GODD levels. So when you get into it, it's going to be a whole learning curve like this, actually for Diablo. WoW is kind of down for learning curve. The learning curve actually is reversed on it. Well, it's not, it's a mental learning curve. It's up a little like this. TF – Team Fortress – is a learning curve of a little bit higher.

And GODD is almost a straight up learning curve. It's so difficult. So we want to prepare you for that. Once you're in it, you'll start using that like a cleansing effect every day, so you'll be actually cleaning your teeth every day with the GODD Levels. So I want to get you up to that point where you can at least do that much. Then, we'll also show you how to use the ESD loops and the ESD movements for the same purpose of cleansing. That keeps you clean. When you keep clean of biological imperatives, when you get your biologicals off, you'll discover that the waking state is so much easier to actualize, to activate. But you've got to get those biologicals off first. That's the overburden that's keeping you down, keeping you suppressed.

I offer you that workshop. You tell me when you want that workshop. You name the time and the place. I'll be there. Okay, don't forget . . . no matter what anybody else ever tells you, YOU CAN WAKE! Do it with me. No matter what anybody ever tells you . . . .

All: YOU CAN WAKE!

All right. WAKING IS. That's a t-shirt! Okay, let's go!

E.J. Gold, Seeing The Invisible, Charcoal on Arches 1990

E.J. Gold, Music of the Heavens, Charcoal on Arches, 1987

CHAPTER 1

The Situation

**The impartial observation of the limits of life in a fish tank
can provide us with an important clue as to the real nature
of our planetary situation and a basis for asking ourselves
what the meaning and purpose of life can be.**

If we take the time to closely observe a fish tank, we will
notice that the tank is a closed environment, a totally
independent ecosystem which depends upon a delicate balance
of interior equilibrium and interspecies order. The fish tank is
a miniature world in itself.

Each living creature in the tank has its place and function,
and everything is connected to everything else.

The plants are compatible with the pH balance of the water
solution and they are neither too big, nor too small; their root
system is adapted to the bottom soil so they neither float away
nor rot.

1

The fish, too, have their necessary and inescapable roles and functions in the social and ecological hierarchy of the tank.

They are selected—by human beings living outside the tank —according to an artificial mutual compatibility; deadly enemies would not survive for very long in a small sealed environment.

Some of the species and members of species are dominant, some are submissive in relation to the others; still others seem to avoid getting involved in any relationship with the other fish.

Some fish live near the surface of the tank, never venturing to the bottom; some remain at the bottom for the whole of their lives, and some live in between.

The bottom scavengers, usually suckers and catfish, are the garbage collectors of the tank; they eat the rotting materials which have filtered down from the top, and at the same time they clean the rocks and the glass, thus ensuring that harmful moss and lichens will not proliferate and upset the delicate balance of the tank.

Those that live in the middle such as the sharks, redbellies and guppies, manage to live off what the fish at the top have not eaten as it was introduced into the tank from outside by a human hand.

Some fish will be quicker than others, and consume more food and expend more energy than others.

Those who live near the surface, such as the goldfish and redfins, will always be the first served, so they, in a certain sense, dominate the others. Others like the eel will seem perfectly at ease anywhere in the tank—top, middle or bottom.

A few creatures in the tank will seem totally oblivious to all its activities. The turtle will quietly go about its business and basically ignore and keep away from the other inhabitants of the tank. However distant it may seem to our observing glance, it will nevertheless be in harmony with everything and everyone in the tank.

In spite of all the apparent activity in the tank, its dwellers have extremely limited contact with each other; not only do they not move around from one level to another, but they have no need or means to share whatever information they happen to acquire subjectively about the tank they inhabit.

The top dwellers know very little about life at the bottom, and the bottom dwellers know very little about life at the top.

Still, let us suppose that, for those who are hungry to learn, information will be available, somehow slowly making its way around from fish to fish and from species to species, filtering almost unnoticed through their isolation, but that it is seldom pieced together by any one fish into a coherent picture.

In looking at this sealed environment, we cannot help but be struck by the fact that we are looking at an entire self-contained world, surrounded by an ocean of air, just as our planet is self-contained in the sense that it is a harmonious environment, and it is also suspended in an ocean—an ocean of space, a near-vacuum even less dense than our planetary atmosphere.

Just as the fish are tied forever to their denser liquid

atmosphere, and would die without it, we are also tied to our gaseous atmosphere and would soon die if we were unable to breathe it.

We may be very surprised to see quite clearly from our vantage point outside the tank that, although this miniature world is surrounded by our world and is a part of it, it is more or less completely cut off from any other similar world outside itself, including its larger relatives, the oceans, seas, and lakes, and that, just as in our world, the inhabitants of the fishtank are completely ignorant of anything outside their little world, and cannot even perceive objects and events outside the tank in our world, the nearest dimension just once-removed beyond their own.

Unless some accident or very unusual discovery happens to occur in the course of events, the fish will remain totally unaware of anything beyond the tank. They will continue to believe that their tank is the beginning and end of all possible worlds and never question their existence in the tank.

For all practical purposes they will be right, insofar as they are utterly incapable of participating actively and consciously in an outside world; however, if the routine in this next highest dimension is in any way disrupted, their own world will suffer the consequences on a very large scale.

What might be a small disturbance in our world will be felt as a major upheaval in their own world.

The fish in a tank are utterly dependent on humans for their survival. If it were not for humans, no food would be introduced into the tank, and the pumps and filters would soon cease to operate. This clearly establishes the precariousness of their situation, and if any of the fish were observant, would

4

provide them with an important clue about their world.

They have no way of knowing that there could be much more room to swim around if they were not in the tank, and they have no way of making observations which would lead them to question the invisible barrier against which they continually bump.

They have nothing with which to compare their experience. How could they understand that the invisible walls are not the edge of creation, only a glass partition?...

These observations lead us to ask ourselves what the real meaning of life could possibly be for a fish in the tank. And along the same line of thought, what can be considered a real accomplishment?

E.J. Gold, Other Worlds, Charcoal on Arches 1987

CHAPTER 2

What to Do?

If our world is actually related to other worlds, then we must ask ourselves what we can accomplish that would be significant and of objective value and consequence beyond its limited confines.

What could a fish trapped in a fish's body with a fish's mind, doomed to a relatively short life in a sealed tank possibly do that would truly be significant and of consequence not only subjectively, but far beyond the small satisfactions of his small world?

If the fish were able to build a sandcastle, for example, would it really have accomplished anything of objective significance? Would it change anything for the fish? Would its fate be improved? Could it hope for anything better for itself?

If the fish were able to leave the tank and go back to the ocean, would this really change anything for them? Once they were back in the ocean, should we suppose they would they have any real hopes of a better life?

They might die from sheer shock, from the trauma of adapting to a new environment; they might no longer be able to fend for themselves, and survive on their own...

But what would be the point of returning to the ocean? What would be the nature of something better for them?

Some of the fish, realizing the futility of their lives, might focus on the central factor of their lives—the food. They might decide that it would be worthwhile to study the food, and after a while they might decide to give dissertations and workshops on how to properly select and eat food; whether to eat it as it is falling, or to catch it while it is still floating on the top, or wait until it reaches the bottom.

But what would this preoccupation with food mean, ultimately? Would they be any better off in a real sense? Even if their health and well-being were slightly improved, would their lives be any more significant? Would they have achieved a higher purpose?

Suppose that some of the fish, having suddenly remembered a bit of information their mothers gave them as minnows, decided to expound the merits of deep breathing, or rapid breathing, or perhaps slow, rhythmic breathing—how should we regard this effort on their part to relieve the tedium of life in the tank?

If the fish decided to organize themselves, to establish committees to take care of various interspecies problems, tank territory problems, minnow-care problems, and they formed a quorum to elect a leader who could give a definite direction to their lives, would this really change anything for them besides complicating their daily routine, and immersing them even further in their limited concerns about life in the tank?

If some of the fish became historians, setting themselves the aim of describing what life is like in the tank, for the benefit of future generations of fish, what would this really accomplish?

Or perhaps one or two of the more intelligent fish had serious thoughts about the meaning and significance of life in the tank, and shared these thoughts with other fish, not in the spirit of inquiry, but as authorities...of what real benefit would this be to themselves and others?

If the fish who lived at the top described to the fish who lived at the bottom what life was like near the surface, then already some of them would have an expanded view of the situation. If the bottom fish described life at the bottom to those who lived at the top, then again this information could expand horizons.

Suppose all the fish shared whatever information they had about their world, this again could certainly help them have a better view of their overall situation.

By clearly reporting what they were able to observe in their own territory, and organizing the data reported to them by members of their own and other species, they might even begin to glimpse the artificiality and limits of the tank...They might even begin to guess the nature of their world in relation to another, much larger, world of which it was only a very small and insignificant part...

What if one of the fish—let us call this fish Redfin— suddenly grasped his situation and distinctly understood the fact that he was a fish in a tank, and that he also was able to make some accurate guesses about the nature of life in the tank...

Suppose that from this he was able to deduce the existence of life outside the tank; that the world inside the tank was very limited, that in fact it was only one world among many—one way of living and breathing among many possible ways of living and breathing.

Is there any hope that he could accomplish something of objective value, considering that he is a fish confined to a fishtank, perhaps forever?

What could he accomplish inside the tank, a sealed artificial environment from which he could never hope to escape and outside which he could not hope to survive if he did manage to escape? What could he really do that would have greater consequences than just change something about his life in the tank?

If he has evaluated the situation, he must understand that he will never escape the tank, and that nothing he can do in the tank in the ordinary sense will have any real consequences in the larger sense, and yet he is not satisfied with the small momentary pleasures which seem to satisfy the other fish, and he realizes that after he dies, his life will have no meaning for him, nor in the long run, for anything or anyone else.

But even though he cannot change the fact that he will live as a fish, and someday inevitably die as a fish, in a sealed tank, and that his life ultimately will have no meaning in the historical or geological sense, can he do something that would really change anything about his situation?

To begin with, he would have to be able to piece together everything that was known about the tank, for which he would be dependent upon information gathered from other, generally undependable, sources, because although he is interested in obtaining a whole picture of the tank, he is still a fish of a certain species and can only extend his explorations so far and no farther.

He is dependent on information from others because his own personal knowledge about the tank, gathered by himself, would be far too limited to make any serious deductions.

But even if the secondhand information is distorted in some respects, he could gather sufficient data to enable him to obtain an overall view of the tank and actually grasp the fact that the tank was artificial, had definite limits, and that its purpose for existing—and his—was probably decorative, although this last idea might not occur to him for some time.

In addition, he could gather information that would imply that a fixed type and amount of food suddenly appeared in the tank at more or less definite and predictable intervals, and moreover, that other elements of tank maintenance seemed to be in the hands of some unknown agency, acting from above.

By putting together all available knowledge and combining it with his own experience, he might come to surprising results.

For example, as he remembered his experience of breathing at the surface of the tank, he might suddenly realize that he had sampled something on the other side of the water— perhaps an ocean of air just like his own liquid atmosphere, only far less dense—which he recognized as an atmosphere which was definitely poisonous and deadly to his continued survival.

He would perhaps slowly remember that he had actually

dimly perceived this alien atmosphere long ago, but never paid much attention to it or gave it much significance because it was so unpleasant...

At the same time he would know that he could not survive on the other side of the tank because he had tasted the atmosphere surrounding it. He would know that as a fish he was not equipped for life outside the tank.

He would soon come to realize that, even if he could leave his miniature world and enter the higher dimension he had discovered, he clearly could not survive life in the higher dimension.

So by gathering information in this way, Redfin could eventually discover the limits of the tank, his world, his dimension.

He could set himself the task of determining very precisely the nature of these limits and by so doing, he could definitely, with the right perception of the available facts, clearly grasp the fact that the tank—his own dimension—was actually part of our world—which would be, in relation to his world, another, higher dimension.

If Redfin were able to deduce the existence of this higher dimension surrounding the tank, and he also knew that the walls of the tank were transparent, he would realize that the higher dimension must be visible to him—must always have been visible to him—if he could only readjust his vision to penetrate beyond what he knew to be the limits of his universe.

He would be able to realize that the higher dimension had been visible all along; that he had always seen it, but because his vision automatically rejected and rendered invisible everything beyond the transparent walls of the tank, he had not understood what he had been seeing, and had been unaware of its significance.

If he knew that the walls of the tank were transparent and that therefore he had seen but rejected perceptions of the higher dimension all along, he would understand that he was unable to perceive it because of a psychological barrier.

He would realize at once that he would first have to break through this artificial barrier created by his own mind before he could directly perceive the higher dimension.

He would see that, because his mind was conditioned to reject perceptions of the higher dimension, he might have trouble recognizing objects and events beyond the tank, but if he could overcome his automatic mental and emotional rejection, he would be able to obtain definite firsthand evidence of the higher dimension outside the tank.

His vision is prevented by psychological convention from penetrating beyond the glass walls of the tank, but if he dares to break with convention, it need not remain confined to his own little world.

But even if he knows that his vision is blocked by artificial mental and emotional barriers and that in fact he has always seen but rejected the perceptions of the next higher dimension, which he now deduces to exist all around him, how is he to come to actually see it? His vision is conditioned to the confines of the tank.

What unusual movement will be necessary for him to be able to turn around and see with his own eyes the world which has surrounded the tank all his life and which, if he could only open his eyes, would appear to him at this very moment?

13

E.J. Gold, Tet Offensive '63 , Charcoal on Arches 1987

CHAPTER 3

Our Potential for Inner Evolution

The key to accomplishing something of objective value lies in our potential for inner evolution; special methods can teach us how to use our body, mind and emotions to transform our essential selves.

Eventually if Redfin were successful at readjusting his vision, he would see something—and even if he were utterly unable to comprehend what he saw, he would have obtained a definite glimpse of a higher dimension beyond his own.

His vision of the higher dimension would certainly lead him to question in a very serious way all that he had so far taken for granted and what once seemed so obvious to him...

Let us assume that he already knows many new things: that his world or dimension is only one among many, that life in at least the most immediate higher dimension would be impossible for him, and that in a certain sense, because his

15

possible evolution is independent of his surroundings and his situation, escape to a higher dimension is both totally irrelevant and unnecessary.

He might see something as astounding as a living creature as big as his entire universe. If he could understand that this creature was part of a dimension once removed from his own, he could deduce from this that there were other higher dimensions as well, perhaps an infinite number of dimensions all totally inaccessible to him, but even if inaccessible, he could, from the standpoint of his own lower dimension, deduce from the evidence of at least one higher dimension, the existence of a highest dimension, the dimension of the Absolute.

He might not realize it at first, but not only is the next higher dimension visible from his own, but all higher dimensions as well are in plain sight if he can make the adjustment in vision which would enable him to bypass the machine's natural rejection of their perception.

He cannot learn much about these higher dimensions, but since they seem impossibly remote at the moment, it makes little difference to him in his immediate dilemma, but their very existence and the possible existence of the highest dimension give him the only clue he really needs to achieve his own transformation and evolution.

Redfin might immediately decide to tell everyone about his discovery and ask others what they know or have deduced about it. He would not think this strange—after all, the higher dimension is easily visible just outside the transparent barrier of glass, requiring only a minor adjustment of vision to penetrate and render invisible the glass barrier which occludes its perception.

Why, the moment he points it out, he reasons to himself, they ought to be able to see it for themselves!

In his first excitement, he might dart this way and that about the tank, telling all those who were willing to listen— whether out of curiosity, or the desire to collect more material for gossip, or out of a sincere desire to learn something—what he had so unexpectedly discovered about their situation, and how urgent it seemed to him to act on it.

He would soon discover to his complete puzzlement and seething frustration, that very few—if any—of the other fish were at all interested in what he had to say.

Some would be too busy and preoccupied with the business of the tank, some would not have the intelligence to understand what was being conveyed, others would not care to be distracted from their amusements, and others still would just not want to be bothered with something out of their comfortable routine.

The fact is that most of them simply would not care about the limitations of their world, and certainly would have no interest in the existence of other higher and encompassing dimensions, even if they were easily observable.

Not only would they find the idea incomprehensible and disturbing, but they would have no idea what to make of it. From their own view of themselves in relation to their world, they would be unable to find any value or potential to themselves in this.

And how upset they would be with Redfin! What if he were right, and there was another higher dimension outside the tank? What would be the point in knowing about it?

And when they contrasted their own petty lives against the background of an incomprehensibly vast reality...

How insignificant it would make them feel, especially if he could prove that an unthinkably greater being lived in this higher dimension and fed them, and looked over them, and seemed interested in their affairs, and who not only took care of their most immediate needs, but who, according to many first-hand witness reports, actually lifted them up out of the tank into some sort of heaven—possibly Redfin's higher dimension—after they died.

What could Redfin do, if he suddenly realized that he was alone with his new-found truths—that there was little or no hope of reaching anyone else, and if he did, what he had discovered would be inevitably distorted into some religious belief or psychological theory.

He would have little or no hope of obtaining any real answers from the other fish, at the same time he would not have grown too far beyond what he had been before, and he would still feel the weight of the old, lost illusions...

What aim could Redfin set himself after this shocking discovery? What might be demanded of him? And would he, as he is, be able to answer these demands?

Could he ever really hope to have an objective view of life outside the tank? Could he ever understand what it means to be in a lower dimension staring a higher dimension right in the face?

Even if he succeeded in understanding these things, how could he use this information to produce in himself something which would enable him to become something entirely different, something which would free him from his ordinary fate in life as a fish in a tank?

He knows that whatever he might be able to learn, guess or deduce about the higher dimension itself would be irrelevant to his immediate aim.

He would soon come to realize that the most important thing for him at the moment would be just to know that higher dimensions exist, and that they would be visible to him at this very moment if he knew how to overcome his psychological rejection of their perception and, knowing this, he might also come to realize that this rejection of their perception is somehow tied to his present state.

Eventually he might also deduce the possibility of changing himself in some way—certainly not physically, so it would have to be psycho-emotionally and perhaps in other more subtle ways as well—so that he could serve a higher dimension without actually living in it.

If he were able to see the higher dimension, and had been able to deduce the possibility of change, he would soon see that his only chance for evolution would be to somehow make himself useful to a higher dimension and thus to a higher set of laws to which he would be forced to adapt.

Evolution would thus become a compelling necessity, without which he would never rise above the vague wish to evolve beyond his present condition.

The first glimpse of a higher dimension could serve to provide the only clue that he would really need to understand exactly how he could raise himself from his ordinary destiny as a fish in a tank, and use his life for some objective purpose, a purpose far beyond his life in the tank, but eventually if he hoped to go further, he would have to achieve more than just an occasional glimpse.

If Redfin were to accomplish anything of objective value, he would have to discover that his only recourse would be to throw himself onto his own potential for inner evolution, and that this would involve, at least in the beginning, the necessity of overcoming the natural biological rejection of the perception of the higher dimension.

Redfin might, if he were thrown back on his own resources, discover some method which would utilize his only real possession, the only thing which can never be taken from him throughout his life in the tank—his own body, with its mind, sensations and emotions.

He might further be able to deduce a method of using his body, mind and emotions for his own evolution—while still remaining a fish in a tank—and he could conceivably, if he is very fortunate, also discover a use for his life, if he could find a way to activate his own inner evolution.

In doing so, he would inevitably discover in the course of events a much higher purpose than his own small purposes, which would, if he were able to bring himself into alignment with it, raise his whole life beyond the petty confines of the tank, and place him on a path which would require that he perform tasks of real significance, not necessarily of significance to himself.

He might not even understand the aim and purpose of his activities for a very long time, but his life would be of genuine significance to something much greater than himself.

In the course of his new discoveries, he might also come to realize that a part of himself is definitely not Redfin—not a fish in a tank—and that the evolution of this other, ordinarily unseen and unsuspected part of himself, is his only real chance to raise himself beyond his otherwise futile existence.

And why shouldn't he be able to discover this unseen part of himself? Hasn't he already discovered a higher dimension outside the tank—a dimension which, if he had known how to look and what to look for, he would have seen all along?

He knows now that he need only turn his gaze inward and break through the psychological barriers which reject the perception of the unseen part of himself to find an essential self which is not the fish in the tank, and which he understands now would have been equally visible all his life, had he only known what he was looking for, and had he known how to recognize it when he found it.

He has found a way to transcend his ordinary destiny as a living decorative object; he knows and understands that he can never escape the tank as long as the fishy part of himself lives, and yet, if he understands the method of personal evolution, the use of the body, mind and emotions as a transformational apparatus for the essential self, he has no immediate need to leave the tank in order to achieve his transformation and evolution, nor to change his outer life as a fish in any way.

A fish he is, and a fish he will remain; what has really changed is his potential to take a much more meaningful place in the larger scheme of things.

Like Redfin, perhaps we have already measured the limits of the tank, evaluated our lives in relation to the tank and to the other fish in the tank, and come to recognize clearly that nothing we do in the ordinary way, that is, in relation to our environment or to the other fish, will be of any real consequence.

Let us assume that we know this and, like Redfin, we have had momentary glimpses of the next higher dimension from which we have deduced the existence of an Absolute dimension, and that from this we have further recognized the futility of life in the ordinary sense.

If we have seen that much—and we would not now be drawn to these ideas if we had not seen at least this—we would then be able to deduce the existence of an unseen part of ourselves and its potential for some form of evolution using the body, mind and emotions as a transformational apparatus. But what, specifically, are we to do now?

E.J. Gold, Sweetly I Sleep, Charcoal on Sennelier, 1989

E.J. Gold, Facing The Truth, Charcoal on Arches 1996

CHAPTER 4

The Human Biological Machine as a Transformational Apparatus

Contrary to popular belief, inner transformation does not produce behavioral and psychological results that can be easily recognized from the outside. Real results are of an entirely different nature.

We are in a way victims of several diseases of civilization, one strong symptom of which is the characteristic intellectual arrogance of our present culture.

Intellectual arrogance can be defined as the assumption that we fully understand an idea the first time we hear it, just because we happen to recognize the words and think we understand their deep, subtle meanings.

We should recognize clearly that it may be many years, if ever, before we arrive at a complete understanding of these

25

ideas, and even then we will only arrive at this understanding if we have personally used these ideas and measured them against observable and definable results in ourselves.

What we as civilized human beings may have trouble understanding is that ideas are fully grasped only when they reflect a corresponding inner change; we come to understand only what exists in ourselves, and nothing exists in ourselves which we have not taken within, digested and deeply considered with much more than just the mental apparatus.

In order to fully understand an idea, we must have actually put it to use, becoming familiar with all its subtle ramifications and connections with other ideas already formed in us through previous experience.

New ideas, particularly ideas considered in this preparatory work, will not fit into any known category. It is imperative that we come to understand that these ideas are not available in the mainstream, and that we have never actually heard them before, even though we may think we are somewhat familiar with them through other sources.

We will consider several important ideas in this introduction to the Work and, as we hear these ideas, we must remember that we do not understand them completely, and that, although we might clarify a point or two, we can never completely understand them just by talking about them or thinking about them.

In our beginning work, we will turn our first attention toward the body, with its mental, emotional and motor apparatuses, which when taken as a whole, is called in this system, the human biological machine.

Although it has countless inner subjective states which may

give the impression of an unapproachable complexity, the human biological machine has only two definite objective states which are of any real interest to us in the transformational sense. The machine is either in the waking state or the sleeping state.

In the ordinary course of life, apart from momentary accidental awakenings, the machine is asleep, and during this sleeping state, it exercises its own will upon the situation, and at the same time, its higher transformational functions are not activated.

In the sleeping state, its attention is completely fixated on its own inner subjective thoughts, emotional states and sensations, or on those distractions and attractions outside itself which happen to impose themselves through the thick veil of its subjective fixation on itself, which is the real meaning of the ancient myth of Narcissus.

Our experiences in the search for real meaning in our lives have all more or less been the same. In spite of a long and sincere search for serious knowledge, we never seemed to be able to find real answers, practical answers...We were never able to find ideas that worked and that actually produced measurable results.

Most of us eventually came to the conclusion that people who were already in the Work had for some reason decided to form a conspiracy to be obscure and mysterious.

But the pitiful truth is that very few people, even very famous and highly acclaimed directors of work communities, actually know the basic fact of work: that only an awakened human biological machine can produce a transformational effect upon the essential self—that part of us which is not the machine.

The majority of work communities are founded on the basis that it is the essential self which is asleep and which must be aroused from sleep. Because they remain unaware of the essential self's identification with the sleep of the machine, and the machine's potential as a transformational apparatus only when in the waking state, they have no hope of achieving any authentic transformation.

Few people know this important secret, yet even knowing this secret does not guarantee that they know everything necessary for the transmission of these ideas; they may not know how to communicate the ideas to somebody else, and in any case, they may only know the ideas mentally, having never actually applied them in a practical way to themselves. A real teacher ought to be able and willing to demonstrate his or her own transformation and waking state, and not just talk about it. Talk is cheap, and anyone who has listened to a few lectures and seems sincere, can convince the ignorant.

If we have seriously searched for something like a school, it is obvious to us that ordinary methods cannot produce anything other than ordinary results, and that only the extraordinary methods of a school, methods which are unknown and unavailable in the mainstream of ordinary life, can produce school results.

In this sense, it can be understood that a school is a community of people gathered together for the purpose of awakening their machines and using the awakened machine for the purpose of transformation toward their possible evolution.

These early definitions of a school, of work, sleep,

awakening and transformation are to be taken as temporary and incomplete ideas. We will further define the ideas of sleep, awakening and transformation in the course of this introduction to work with a school.

If the awakening of the machine and the resulting transformation of the essential self could be produced in any ordinary way, then anyone who has ever lived an ordinary life should have been transformed and there would be no necessity for schools.

And yet, schools exist, and if we know nothing else about the Law of Conservation of Energy, we do understand that nothing exists without necessity.

We also should have deduced that, if transformation produced results which we could recognize in someone else, then we might think that every genius who ever lived ought to have achieved transformation. But even the greatest human beings in the whole parade of history have failed to achieve transformation in any real sense of the word.

But how can we even think of coming to a school unless we understand right from the very beginning the foundation, the basis, the deepest premise of the Work: that the human biological machine—but only in its awakened state—is the transformational apparatus for the possible evolution of the essential self?

When the machine is awake, its attention turns inward toward the essential self, that part of ourselves which is not the machine. When its attention is thus fixated on the essential self, this produces definite transformational effects.

For our very beginning work, we can think of the human biological machine as an alchemical factory which, if it can be

29

awakened from its mechanical sleep, produces the transformation and evolution of the essential self.

The essential self may become drunk with the sleep of the machine, completely identified with it. The essential self may even come to think of itself as asleep, but the fact remains that the essential self is neither awake nor asleep.

How can we see this mysterious essential self?

The human biological machine reflects the presence of the essential self in much the same way a Wilson Cloud Chamber can demonstrate the presence of unseen particles. Although we cannot see the essential self directly, we can see the results of the path it took, its effects on the machine.

The Wilson Cloud Chamber is a device which graphically shows the path, not of what we are measuring, but of something invisible which collided with the something we can see and measure.

We can measure visible particles in the Cloud Chamber, particles which moved because of a transfer of energy that occurred during an impact with something we could not see, and from this deduce a great deal about the thing we cannot see. We can tell quite a bit about this invisible essential self just by measuring its effects.

Like the Cloud Chamber, the human biological machine is a reciprocal biofeedback apparatus in relation to the essential self. Because both the essential self and the machine are electrical in nature, the two fields impinging upon one another produce a third electrical field which can be expressed mathematically. In addition, each field can radically affect the other, which can work to our evolutionary advantage. Later, we will discuss this important idea in detail.

E.J. Gold, The Water Bearer, Charcoal on Rives BFK, 1987

E.J. Gold, Going Where I've Never Been, Charcoal on Arches 1987

CHAPTER 5

Beyond Personal Enhancement

Most psychological methods provide us with a means to achieve personal enhancement by changing behavioral patterns of the "machine". Real transformational methods enable us to achieve objective change by transforming the "essential self" and completely disregarding the effect we have upon others.

In the beginning, we will be concerned almost exclusively with the awakening of the machine from its sleep, a state to which all humans are subject in the ordinary course of life. Our earliest work will be to raise ourselves from the helpless fixation of the machine upon its ordinary organic pursuits.

Even a superficial study of our situation demonstrates clearly that in our present condition, we are utterly powerless to prevent ourselves from being carried along by the machine in these pursuits, the majority of which go completely contrary to our highest aims, aspirations and intentions.

Besides, life in the organic world has taught us to be complacent; why should we pay for life when we can just drift through it in the dark?

Most methods provide a means to change the machine. This is strictly for people who are interested in personal enhancement, in the effect they have upon others. We, on the other hand, are interested in objective change and consequently work to be changed *by* the machine.

But what exactly does it mean, *to be changed*? What is it that is being changed, and for what ultimate purpose? To what use? Most importantly, what is it, exactly, that is undergoing transformation?

We know it is not the machine. The machine is just a kind of factory which produces change. We do not care what the factory looks like, or what others think about it. We are not interested in using the machine as an expression of our personality, which is in fact just another part of the machine.

If we understand the machine's value as a transformational apparatus, we are concerned with the machine and its life only insofar as it produces change in our essential selves, toward our own possible evolution.

Although we can come to know and understand the machine in detail, we cannot change the machine directly, nor do we wish to, once we understand its objective function as a transformational apparatus.

Before we can use any method at all for the awakening of the machine, we must clearly recognize *that it is the machine, and not the essential self which is asleep,* and that only an

34

awakened machine can produce transformation. We must also realize that nobody can activate our machine for us; we must activate it for ourselves.

In the beginning, the essential self cannot exert the will to directly awaken the machine, although it can exercise a special type of will called will-of-attention which has the effect, over a long period of time, of gently awakening the machine just by the inexorable pressure of unremitting attention upon it.

The work of a school will cure us once and for all of this lack of will, by giving us the means to awaken the machine, providing us with new equipment for life.

At its best, the human biological machine should function as a chemical and electrical factory through which we pass in a definite series of processes, entering at one end of the factory in what we call birth, emerging at the other end during the death of the machine as something quite different, in much the same way that any raw material would enter a factory and emerge as a finished product at the other end.

We say in both cases that a transformation has occurred; in the first instance an extraordinary inner transformation visible only to a trained observer, and in the second case, an ordinary transformation visible to the untrained eye.

While in human form we take upon ourselves all the attributes, aspects, and knowledge of a human being. If the machine has been dead during our passage through it, when we leave it at the end of life, we lose everything, all the knowledge and all the experience we had accumulated.

If the electrical force of transformation is activated, the essential self is changed, transformed, so that we retain the knowledge, the attributes, of a human being. But this is true

35

only if we have passed through something *living*, something which has had a definite electrical effect upon our essential self.

If we have passed through something dead, something cold, something lifeless, something dark, the electrical transformational effect is absent. In this case, the essential self emerges at the end of life completely unchanged.

It is a terrible waste of the opportunity of human life, a genuine sin, to have failed to use the human biological machine for our possible evolution.

Most people feel that they are wasting their lives, and at one time or another recognized that if they really wanted to, they could find out quite easily the real purpose of human life.

It is not a particularly well-kept secret, and even a superficial search soon reveals the answer. If we understand that most human beings do in fact know that they could know their purpose for existence *but do nothing about it*, we understand the basis of sleep, which is sometimes formulated as, *the secret keeps itself.*

E.J. Gold, Speaking of Myself, Charcoal on Sennelier, 1989

E.J. Gold, Nothing To Hide , Charcoal on Arches 1987

CHAPTER 6

Beginning Work

The purpose of beginning work is to bring the machine into the waking state and to enable it to function as a transformational apparatus. Transformation is not an aim in itself but a stepping stone to a whole new way of life which we seek.

The purpose of the majority of our special exercises is not particularly mysterious. It is the aim of all our beginning work to bring the machine to life, to raise ourselves from its hypnotic and compelling biological fixations, to shake off the coils of desire, our immersion in its wasteful sleep, thus producing from the ordinary human machine a functioning transformational apparatus.

Since the transformational process is cumulative, the periods of awakening add up. In a sense, it makes no difference how often the machine falls back asleep or for how long. Nothing is lost. All we must do is remember to awaken it again by whatever means are necessary to bring it back to life.

The specific activities of the machine are irrelevant in relation to our transformation; what really matters is whether the machine is awake or asleep.

In this sense, we must keep in mind that our real aim is not transformation. Transformation is a stepping stone to the Work, a special way of life which is possible for us only after our essential selves have been transformed, and our machines are more or less stable in the awakened state.

When our transformation is complete, the machine becomes a tool for work. It has cleared itself of those things which made it non-functional as a work tool.

The Work can only be seen and understood through an awakened machine. We cannot see the Work if our machine is asleep, so one of the purposes of awakening the machine is to be able to study the Work.

We should take the opportunity to use the awakened state to study the Work, so that we will know what to do with our transformation once it is achieved.

It is important that we use the few awakened periods available to us, that we not putter them away in pursuits of pleasures of the flesh; that we actually *do* something with them for our possible evolution.

How to best use these periods of awakening is an entirely different question which will be explained in detail later on.

Most of us here are still beginners and should therefore devote ourselves to beginning work. In our present state, before our transformation has occurred, our study is limited to the study and application of various methods of awakening the machine.

It is the task of a school to act as our temporary guide, and to introduce us to the transformational apparatus, our true teacher, to help us develop a working relationship with the machine toward our possible evolution.

To awaken the factory and turn it toward its transformational function requires knowledge—exact knowledge.

We must know exactly which lower and higher motor, reflexive, mental and emotional apparatuses must be activated for each effect in the transformational process.

Although the specific activities of the machine have no relation to its awakening, and awakening cannot be produced by any specific activities, certain special exercises can help us to gain the will necessary to coax two attributes of the essential self into action in order to bring the machine into the waking state.

We will soon discover, as we begin to gather serious conclusive evidence of the machine's sleep, and the exact nature of this sleeping state, that the essential self—which is not in the sleeping state but a state quite apart from anything belonging to the machine—possesses no attributes of its own other than its impartial presence and the simple will-of-attention which, in the early state, is unexercised and therefore weak.

We will also soon realize that in spite of its higher aims and aspirations, the essential self has no will in the ordinary sense by which it can compel the machine to live according to its higher nature.

So we must use what we actually do have in the essential self, the two genuine attributes of the essential self—presence and will-of-attention—to bring the machine into the waking state, and for this we will be forced to develop a strategy, an exact strategy by which we can effectively activate the transformational properties of the human biological machine without also at the same time inadvertently triggering the machine's defense mechanism against the waking state.

We will talk more about this defense mechanism, what it means and how to disarm and de-activate it later, but first we must understand several things.

On the biological level, the human biological machine is a chemical factory just like any other chemical factory, operating under the same basic chemical laws. It is regulated by very small electrical pulses coursing through the myo-neurological system, which is to say, the muscles and nerves.

In addition, we must have some idea of how the factory operates, what it actually is, of what it is capable, and how to make it function as an apparatus for the transformation of energy, the stuff of which our essential selves are made. We will study the machine as a chemical factory in the course of our beginning work. At the same time, we will study it as an electrical field and even as a self-propelled mechanism responding to inner and outer stimuli, conditioned and regulated by several important primate directives and biochemical imperatives which we will discuss in a later talk.

Because the awakened machine is the causative agent of transformation, exercises which are intended to directly produce transformation are not possible, and the results of such exercises are entirely imaginary.

Our exercises are intended strictly for the purpose of bringing the machine into the waking state, from which state it is possible to activate the machine's transformational functions.

If we expect to awaken the machine and activate it as a transformational apparatus, we must develop the higher faculty of *discernment*; we must recognize periods when the machine is awake and, more importantly, periods *when it is not*.

We must use the faculty of discernment to determine whether the machine is awake or asleep, because we must be able to use the time when it is awake.

If we think the machine is already awake, we will not work to awaken it and by acting as if it is awake, we will obtain no real results and could spend our lives producing imaginary results. Also, we could easily hurt ourselves and others by trying to do something in sleep *as if we were awake*.

At the same time, if the machine is awake, we must not waste the awakened state on things of sleep.

If we know for a fact that the machine is asleep, and we also know when the machine is awake, we will be able to apply a variety of methods to produce definite transformational results.

But how can we determine without a doubt whether the machine is awake or asleep?

E.J. Gold, Can You See Me? , Charcoal on Arches 1987

CHAPTER 7

Sheep in Sleep

Because the machine—although fully functional in the ordinary sense—lives its whole life in the sleeping state, our work begins in sleep. We must learn to use the elements of sleep to overcome the machine's defense mechanism against the waking state.

If we realize that our attention is totally immersed in a sleeping machine, we understand that we cannot possibly do things as we would if it were awake.

We must recognize that if the machine is asleep, and we are to work seriously to awaken it, we must begin our work in sleep, using the elements of sleep.

But, even while immersed in identification with the machine's sleep, *if we know that it is the machine* which is asleep, we can use special work methods which are specifically designed to be used in the sleeping state.

Because all work must necessarily begin in sleep—after all, if our machines were already in the waking state, we would have no need for work on ourselves in the first place—we must use all the elements of the sleeping state to overcome the sleeping state: the weaknesses, desires, hallucinations, fixations, organic pursuits of pleasure, and suggestibility of the sleeping machine.

Sleep in itself is not bad. It is our *fixation on sleep* while at the same time thinking that we are awake, which can cause unconscious suffering, and we remain fixated in the machine's sleeping state because we do not know how to overcome the machine's defense mechanism against the waking state. In a short while, we will discuss this idea, but first we must come to understand several ideas which form the foundation for our work to disarm the defense mechanism of the machine against the waking state.

If we are free from the seductive influences of the sleeping state, by which I mean that we are free from our own natural desires for the momentary pleasures and seductions of the sleeping state, we can use them in a different way, which we could call *jiu-jitsu yoga*, using the habits and hungers of the machine to overcome the machine's will to remain asleep.

For this we are forced to come to a school, where we can find an outside guide, a helper, to objectively observe the machine and tell us exactly which leverage to apply.

We cannot depend upon our own mental apparatus for this. It is, after all, just another part of the machine, and if we depend upon it to make its own rules by which we are to guide our work, if we trust the machine to invent methods for its own awakening, its sleep will only become deeper and finally, in the end, we will drown in the machine's dreams.

If we really wish to seriously work toward our possible evolution, we must clearly realize that we are sheep in sleep, that the sleeping machine is a completely mechanical apparatus, responding strictly by reflex to a variety of inner and outer influences.

Should we attempt to work under the assumption that the machine is already awake, then we will not work to awaken the machine.

In addition, there is a greater danger. If we allow ourselves to become victims of a hallucinatory method which provides the illusion and sensations of imaginary awakening, we may try to use work methods which properly belong to an awakened machine.

We can use our attention to watch carefully and intensely everything the machine does. We soon gather enough evidence to convince us without a shred of doubt that it thinks by automatic association, that it can conduct an internal dialog with itself, and respond in very complex patterns to all possible situations without our direction, and even without the participation of our attention, that it knows all the appropriate gestures, all the correct social, intellectual and emotional *protocol*...

To our astonishment, as we study the activities of the machine, we see the hands gesticulating wildly, seemingly with a mind of their own, the mouth issuing proclamations which do not even vaguely resemble our real feelings and attitudes, while the whole machine busily follows the daily routine of life, fanatically obeying artificial and arbitrary schedules and timetables that somebody made up out of the blue, and wallowing in one upset after another about some imaginary trifle or other.

We quickly come to understand the sinister purpose of social ritual; we see how it helps to perpetuate the machine's sleep! We see that life in the ordinary sense is ritualized because a sleeping machine works only for its own survival, and it must continue to function day after day, without a master.

If our work is to really begin in sleep, we must somehow bring ourselves to the realization, with the full impact of truth, that the machine is really asleep; then we will have taken the first real step toward crushing that personal vanity behind which is insecurity, behind which is a deep fear which we can only allow to express itself as vanity, which will not allow us to admit even to ourselves that we have fallen from our higher state, that we have become corrupted by our biological baptism, our total immersion in the sleep of the human machine.

Our vanity convinces us that the machine is awake and supports this illusion with activity, sensation and associative thought.

All arguments against the sleep of the machine which use activities as evidence—how can we go to work every day if the machine is really asleep? How can we hold a decent conversation? How can we cook? How can we play? How can we eat? How can we even dress ourselves if the machine is asleep?—make the mistake of using the ordinary definition of sleep which is different from the special meaning we give to it here.

Let us imagine ourselves to be drunk, and that someone is

trying to convince us that we really are drunk. But how can we be convinced of this? The drunker we are, the more sober we feel!

When the machine is asleep, we cannot be convinced that the machine is asleep. It is even more difficult for someone else to convince us because at the moment they call our attention to the machine's sleep, we become more alert, more on guard and, in spite of ourselves, the machine begins to awaken.

Then, when we relax, sleep begins to reassert itself and once again we think we can make our own rules for ourselves, but the truth is that we cannot even walk a straight line.

If we can only destroy this vanity in ourselves, if we can bring ourselves to actually *know* that the machine is really and truly asleep, we might be able to awaken it.

Using the sensations of the machine, we will try to sense our immersion in the sleep of the machine, even though our mental apparatus lies to itself and to us, that we seem to be awake, to have volition, free will.

If we can only obtain some definite proof that the machine is asleep, then we will know that we are walking around in a dream, just as in the children's rhyme,

"Row, row, row the boat,
Gently down the stream.
Merrily, merrily, merrily, merrily,
Life is but a dream."

49

Before we go any further, we should try to understand what the words of this rhyme actually tell us.

This is not an ordinary children's rhyme. When used in a special way, it can stimulate definite alterations in the brain and nervous system.

If we can separate it from its automatic mental association with children's nursery rhymes, we can see that it was accidentally overheard sometime in the past and that it was at some time, before its degeneration into a play-verse, obviously the product of a school.

Let us see if we can do something right now, to use this disarmingly simple rhyme to help us sense the sleep of the machine.

We should now find a balance point for our machine, a posture in which we feel that we would be able to sit virtually forever. We will park the machine in this posture, and not move it until the exercise is complete.

We will next remove the social mask which is held in place by facial tensions, noticing in passing the extreme amount of energy we ordinarily commit toward the maintenance of this social mask.

We have no need to be social in this situation, and in any case, we need this energy for our work just now, so we should be able to allow ourselves to relax the facial mask, which should go completely limp.

The eyes are to remain open during the whole of this exercise and each time we repeat the rhyme, we will try to sense the sleep of the machine, with a mood of mild astonishment, as would a very young child.

If we hope to enter this special dimension, we must become as children, and re-learn consciously what we have forgotten about ourselves and our experience of the world.

Now, very softly, and in a very relaxed tone we will repeat:

"Row, row, row the boat,
Gently down the stream.
Merrily, merrily, merrily, merrily,
Life is but a dream."

In the same slow cadence, we will repeat this mantram over and over again until the sensation comes over us that it is the machine which is asleep.

In this beginning exercise, we will try to sense the sleep of the machine, using this mantram to remind ourselves that it is not us, but the *machine*, which is asleep.

If the sensation of the sleeping machine goes away, we must try again until the sensation remains.

This exercise is the very beginning foundation of work. If we do not have a good foundation, we cannot build upon it, so we should take the time to realize, to actually sense that the machine is in fact asleep, not just in an abstract philosophical way but in a very real sense.

If we know the machine is asleep, we have one foot on the path. If we can *sense* that the machine is asleep, we have two feet on the path. From then on, at least things cannot get any worse, they can only get better.

51

The sensation of the sleeping machine will make all intellectual argument for work unnecessary.

In our daily life, regardless of the circumstances in which we find ourselves immersed, we must try to actually obtain, and then hold, the sensation of the sleeping machine, at first doing nothing to awaken it directly.

Observation alone will act upon it to awaken it slowly and gently.

We will work to keep this sensation active in some part of our attention all day long, no matter how distracting the activities.

Remember always that it is the machine which is asleep, and that we are not the machine...that we have been drawn down, seduced into the sleep of the machine.

It will take a while to catch on to the idea, but once we do, we will have our first real taste of what it really means to work.

Of course we all have our ordinary obligations and responsibilities, a family to take care of, we go to work, have tax problems...

All of this is useful and we should not try to change it. When we try to change our lives, if we happen to accidentally succeed, we lose the only handholds we have on our work.

It does not matter what we do in life. We do not have the time to allow the machine to settle into a new life and establish whole new patterns. We must live our life as it is, and just begin with this first small step.

We can perform any activity, hold any ordinary job in life, live any way we wish to and, if we just attune ourselves to our sensing, we can begin our work in sleep by gathering the evidence, using a special form of attention called sensing, by which we mean only that we have become intensely aware of the sensations of the machine, to convince ourselves of the sleep of the machine.

Our intellect may tell us that we are awake, but our sensing tells us that the machine is asleep.

Our beliefs may convince us that we are awake, but our sensing tells us that the machine is asleep.

Our vanity may insist that we are awake, but our sensing tells us that the machine is asleep.

Our higher philosophies and religions may insist that we are awake, but our sensing tells us that the machine is asleep.

If we can sense that the machine is asleep, we have taken the first real step toward awakening it.

Until then everything in our lives, especially our work, is imaginary, just fantasy. If we can only sense the machine's sleep in everything we do, no matter how complex, how rapid, how exhilarated or seemingly exalted!

Of course it all begins with the thought, "Is it possible? I have heard a vague rumor that my machine is asleep. Can it really be true?"

This theme will form the inner basis of everything we do in the beginning.

We now have before us our first work, to obtain occasional glimpses of the truth, to gather definite evidence that the machine really is asleep.

E.J. Gold, Mysterious Glance, Charcoal on Arches 1987

CHAPTER 8

Inner Aims

By making our formulation of our inner aims toward transformation more exact, we may eventually develop a real work aim, not something mental and subjective, but an aim which is practical, immediate, accomplishable and which could actually serve a greater, more objective aim.

Even if we were successful in life in the ordinary sense, we probably very quickly realized that the things that we could accomplish in ordinary life simply would not satisfy us in any serious way.

Above all, we became dissatisfied with life as we were more or less forced to live it. We knew that there was more to life, but we didn't know what it might be.

We couldn't have been expected to know exactly how to go about finding what we had vague yearnings for, but we did have a vague ache and dissatisfaction. This feeling of dissatisfaction with ordinary life is the principal reason we come to a school.

There is one common idea among those who come to a school—the real possibility of a life that would be different from the kind of life lived by the majority of human beings, a greater, more exalted life.

In our noble enthusiasm in the earlier stages of our search, we may have originally set out to serve the evolution of humanity, to save the planet from destruction, but we soon discovered, perhaps to our astonishment and frustration, that most human beings not only do not wish evolution, but would fight to the very end to avoid it, and even to prevent us from accomplishing it for ourselves.

We discovered that they are quite satisfied with the aims, pursuits, and pleasures of life as it is, and do not expect any more from life than they have been told to expect. They are happy enough with the petty satisfactions of organic pursuits and the predictability of the daily routine.

They find a grim satisfaction in running to a sale at Macy's or the Bay Company, to get a raise in salary, to go skiing on the weekend, to get a sports car, a color TV and a new vacuum cleaner, to learn a new recipe for apple cake or gingerbread pie, or to see Johnny's report card with straight C's, or to be able to loosen the tie after a long business day, or to dream about hitting the four million dollar lottery.

If we really want to contribute something toward the general evolution of the human race and the planet, then we should remember that we cannot really help anyone else until we have helped ourselves.

Coming to a community means coming to work together as

a group. It does not mean coming to work with a teacher; the teacher is the guest of the community, and remains as a guide for a certain amount of time only.

Eventually, members of the work community will be thrown on their own, although the teacher will then be able to help in other ways.

Everything we have learned so far is information about our purpose for being here. We are accumulating information about how to work. But how to work is not just the accumulation of work ideas. We must come to understand very quickly and very clearly that communicating about the ideas is not actually *using* the ideas, and we came here not just to discuss ideas but to learn to use them.

In our work it is demanded of us that we understand exactly what we are trying to do. The outer form may change radically tomorrow, and yet the underlying thread must remain the same; the sub-text underneath our changing work-forms must remain the same.

When we first come to a school, the question is put to us, why are we here, what do we wish for ourselves, what do we seek here, why do we impose ourselves upon this community?

Our original aims in our work will change, and they may change surprisingly often. There are only two reasons to change our aim.

The first reason is that in the course of pursuing one aim, our vision has grown. We are able to formulate our aim more clearly and more to the point. As we begin to learn, our temporary aim will change with an understanding of the greater purpose of the Work.

When we change our aim, we must be absolutely certain that we are not abandoning the aim just because we feel like giving up. We change aims only when the previous aim no longer serves the greater purpose.

The second reason that we might change our aim is that we have actually accomplished it. We have one great purpose for being in a school and then a variety of smaller aims which serve that greater purpose.

If we were in certain work communities in other countries, and we answered incorrectly when we were asked why we were here, we would be asked to leave the community and, from that day forward, we would never be able to penetrate that community—we would never get past the person who gave the interview at the gate.

We must perfect our aim in order to even gain admittance to many communities where these ideas can be learnt. In a way, it would help us to be turned away from community after community until we had sharpened and formulated our aim exactly, and until we had developed a real aim, something which could actually serve a greater aim, not something subjective and fantastical.

However, in this country, we aren't turned away from community after community. We are accepted with open arms regardless of our vague gropings for meaning in our lives, because we don't have communities with high ethical, high-integrity standards. Only if we express an aim which is actually against the aim of the work community are we asked to leave.

So now teachers are forced to take it upon themselves to educate pupils from the first beginning groanings of discomfort with ordinary life to the formulation of higher aims which could realistically be achieved and applied to this life right now.

In any case, in the beginning we would not have formulated an objective aim for ourselves by ourselves, because the material and equipment for the formulation of a real aim is simply not available in the mainstream information.

So even had we wanted to, even if we had realized that our aim was insufficient, we could not have formulated it better until we came to a school and obtained information about work which is not available in books or in lectures.

We need special help even to understand why we come to a school. But once we do understand what we are trying to accomplish, it is our responsibility to make certain that people in generations following ours also are educated from their first vague discomforts to an understanding of a real aim.

We are also expected to educate others in the underlying facts and understandings which are the basis for this work to the extent that they will not simply repeat what they have heard as an aim, but turn around and educate people who come after them towards an understanding of what it means to work. It is a process of education, not of information.

All along the line the question of our purpose in being in a school will apply, because in the process of accomplishing our greater purpose many smaller aims will come to be formulated.

If these new aims are to be real aims, they must actually be accomplishable.

The nature of our earliest aims is that they do change

according to our understanding. As our understanding grows, our aims will reformulate.

Our very first aim in a school will be a definite, objective school aim which we are expected to accomplish. Before that, all our aims are subjective, based upon hearsay, speculation, vague wonder, some third, fourth and even hundredth generation information, and equally vague yearnings.

From the time we first enter a school until the time we are initiated into the first objective aim, all our aims will be subjective and personal, and it cannot be otherwise.

While the machine is asleep, the only equipment with which we could understand the greater aim is the mental apparatus and the mental apparatus cannot grasp the greater purpose.

The objective aims of our work as a community lead inexorably toward the greater purpose. Each of these aims is accomplishable and the proof of their objectivity is that they are accomplishable.

Perhaps we have developed a sense of a potential for evolution. We thought somehow, somewhere, we believed in a higher form of life, something greater. But without definite evidence this can only be a belief and not something which we could verify in our own experience.

We can imagine that most of us have formulated this belief, that there must be some purpose in life, that there must be more to it than just an endless round of pleasure and pain and pursuit of this attraction, and immersion in that distraction, and so on.

To answer this belief would require that we were able to somehow comprehend the greater purpose.

E.J. Gold, Phantom After-Image of the Phenomenal World
Charcoal on Rives BFK, 1996

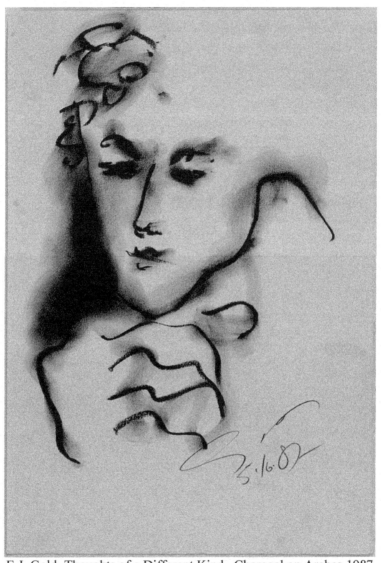

E.J. Gold, Thoughts of a Different Kind , Charcoal on Arches 1987

CHAPTER 9

Study of the Machine

Although we are separate from the machine, we have become hypnotized, immersed in the sleeping state of the machine. One of the purposes of studying the machine is to gather evidence which can help us define the exact nature of this sleep.

The idea that the machine is asleep does not automatically call for belief or faith, because we can easily see for ourselves that the machine is asleep.

Although as essential beings we have separate existence apart from the machine, we have become distracted from our native state which lies far beyond space and time, hypnotically attracted to the machine by some glittering fascination, and we are presently held in its grip by the power of sensation and emotion, entirely immersed in its sleep, and as a result of our total identification with the life of the machine, partaking—

whether willingly or unwillingly—of its sleeping state.

Actually, in a sense, this situation is fortunate for us because, although we may find our life in the machine to be the cause of much needless suffering, it also provides us with the opportunity for transformation, which would otherwise be impossible without the machine's functioning as a transformational apparatus.

In its present state, the human biological machine functions entirely by reflex, answering with its mental, emotional and motor apparatuses the various stimuli presented by the environment and even by the machine's own imaginings and accidental stimulations of memory and mental simulations of possible events which seldom happen as the machine projects and extrapolates them.

We can learn how to see and sense the machine's sleep, and we can gather incontrovertible evidence of the machine's sleeping state beyond a shadow of a doubt, evidence strong enough to stand up in a court of law.

Study of the machine's sleeping state can also serve a second purpose, helping us to define the exact nature of this sleep.

But first of all, before we can even set out to gather evidence of any kind about the machine, we must agree that we do in fact live our lives in a human biological machine.

We must see that, although we have spent our whole lives immersed in total identification with the machine, and the very fibre of our beings has been since birth inextricably woven into the life of the machine, offering plenty of opportunities for study, we have never actually studied the machine and its life.

But it is not enough to just study the machine in the ordinary way, that is, identified with the machine. This would be the same as the machine studying itself. We must learn somehow to study the machine objectively, from outside, in much the same way that an anthropologist would study any other primate—and ultimately, the human biological machine is a primate, with more or less the same primate directives and biological imperatives common to the species—in its natural habitat.

If we cannot agree to these two beginning ideas, then everything that follows is useless, and we might as well go somewhere else where we can hear what we want to hear—perhaps some nice, comforting spiritual mythology—in our never-ending search for the meaning of life, because we will have no further possibility here.

In the beginning of our study of the machine, our first definition of sleep will be that it is *not awake*, whatever that means...and we will begin to define this sleeping state in depth as we proceed, so its meaning will definitely change as we penetrate more and more deeply into these ideas.

In addition, we may know a little something about what it means for the machine to be not asleep, because we may have experienced glimpses of the awakened state from time to time, even if only briefly.

In any case, we know or we have guessed that there is another state very different from the ordinary state, which is possible for the machine, and which leads to another, very different multi-dimensional experience of life than that to which we have become accustomed.

We also know from our own experience that we do not

ordinarily live in this different state, although we may think of this exalted state as real life, as we and the machine ought to live it if we only could.

We also know that if we have experienced this state—let us call it the waking state—we have experienced it only briefly and partially, and then fallen from it for some inexplicable reason, into a state of comparative darkness, a dark and gloomy dungeon of miserable existence, just a shadow of what we saw to be possible.

To our utter astonishment, we come to realize that everyone else regards this dark and gloomy sleeping state as quite acceptable and even comfortable and agreeable.

We eventually come to understand that our first faltering steps into the waking state are only the beginning of real awakening.

But to our disappointment, we soon find that our first objective aim in a school is not, as we would expect, to awaken the machine, but to allow the machine to remain in the sleeping state while we gather evidence to satisfy ourselves that we do indeed live in a machine, and that the machine is definitely asleep.

Some of the evidence of sleep which we gather will be indirect. For example, we may accidentally stumble into a state where we see that the machine is alive, that it has awakened, even if only momentarily and accidentally.

We can deduce from this that until now, since the ordinary state is very dark and dense in comparison, the machine must have been asleep.

We begin to discover the horrifying truth—that in spite of

our strong wish to remain awake, we do not know how to maintain the waking state, and we are forced time and time again to watch helplessly as the sensitized perceptions and sensations close down, and the machine falls back once again under the cloak of darkness.

We speak of the sleeping and waking states in terms of perceptions and sensations because it is a machine-state. Because it is a machine state and the machine has two definite and distinct experiences which are measurable by its senses and sensations, the difference between the two states of waking and sleeping are very clear.

In one state we really see, hear, feel, taste, touch, know, remember. All our senses and mental and emotional functionings are clarified and magnified, thousands of times.

In the sleeping state, we live in darkness, we feel disconnected, harsh, angular, trapped and isolated; we live and breathe in darkness. This is a good beginning definition of sleep in relation to waking.

We can gather direct evidence of the sleeping state while in the sleeping state, because we know that our present state is nothing like what we remember of the glimpses we had of what it was to really be alive in the machine. Of course, as we remember that we are presently in the sleeping state, the machine will inevitably begin to awaken, thus interfering momentarily with our direct observation of its sleep.

In our little glimpses of the awakened state, because they are only glimpses, and therefore momentary and incomplete, we should remember that our experiences of these states are imperfect.

Secondly, we should realize that, because the machine was

not fully awake during these glimpses of awakening, the machine still exerted its will, and because the machine was not fully awake, and vestigial traces of the sleeping state remained somewhat active to a greater or lesser degree, we inevitably experienced some discomfort which would not be part of a complete waking state.

This initial discomfort during the process of entering the waking state from the sleeping state is the principal reason we fall back into the sleeping state.

In our first glimpses of the awakened state, because we were identified with the sleep of the machine, we must have felt some apprehension, a feeling of impending doom, of being on the top of a roller coaster that was about to let go, or of having been pulled back on a slingshot, just at the point of hurtling through a corridor toward some unknown destination.

We didn't know what was going to happen if we allowed ourselves to go all the way, but we *can* understand this experience; we can know exactly what will happen if we allow ourselves to be carried all the way through the experience, through what the ancients called *the Cave.*

We can make an almost exact analogy to the process of entering the waking state from the sleeping state with the examination of a similar situation.

Almost all of us have had the experience of waking in the middle of the night and finding that one of our arms has gone to sleep.

As the blood began to pump back into the limp, dead and useless arm, we may have had the definite impression that we were about to have a heart attack and die.

This is a very important experience because it produces exactly the same sensation as does the awakening machine.

In the sleeping state, the whole machine, including its emotional and mental apparatuses, perceptions, senses and sensations, are completely numb.

We can barely see, we can barely hear, we can barely sense; in a sleeping machine, although our activities may deceive us, we live life at the absolute minimum.

As we begin to massage the machine awake, the tingling sensation becomes too much to bear, so we return to the same state as before and it becomes blissfully numb again.

This is a nearly perfect analogy of what happens to us in the awakening process. We may not have the courage to continue the process of awakening past the point of discomfort.

Certain alarming sensations will definitely occur as the machine begins to awaken: tingling, falling, vertigo, dropping, collapsing, exploding, expanding inside a skin that is stretched too tight, pins and needles, flaming, curling, shortening and lengthening, agitation, weakness, confusion, coldness, sweating, restlessness.

We may recognize these symptoms as the same symptoms which signal the death of the machine and, in a way, the waking state is very much like the death of the machine, because in the waking state, the machine has lost face, in the sense that it no longer has the force to impose its own will upon the situation, and even more importantly, its negative emotions, which provide it with a sense of continuity, have inexplicably vanished.

When the machine first comes to life, we may find the

experience too excruciating, too emotionally, mentally and physically painful, too exhausting, and we may decide to allow the machine to fall back into sleep.

Eventually, if the machine remains in the sleeping state, gangrene will set in and the machine will die. This is the chief cause of ordinary death. If the machine were awake, it would also eventually die, but not in the same way.

The machine is so near death when it is asleep, that when death comes, we will hardly notice it, and it won't be so bad.

But when death comes to a living machine, the difference is so much greater that we will, in fact, be acutely aware of its passing. Because we are alive, life is more precious to us and death will be that much more poignant. We can consider this as a warning. Perhaps it is better to remain in the near-death state of sleep.

We will try to recall the exact sensation—or lack of it—when we woke up in the middle of the night, to discover that one of the arms had fallen asleep. The arm is completely limp, totally limber. It has absolutely no motion, no sensation; we may see it as something which is literally dead, some strange object dangling from the shoulder. Our first thought in that situation must have been that it may never come back to life.

We want to recall the full mental, emotional and sensing memory of that limp, limber dead arm and realize that our whole machine is now in the equivalent condition in relation to its possible awakened state.

When we awaken the machine, it will not be near death, but other machines will be near death, limp, limber, closed, running automatically in darkness and this in itself will also be terrifying.

Perhaps we have had a glimpse of people as automatons, empty puppets, running on mechanically, so near death as to be all-but-dead...

What keeps the machine in sleep is our fear of the discomfort of awakening. This is the real meaning of inertia. But what is it that keeps us—the essential self, which is not the machine—immersed in the sleep of the machine?

Remember what it was like to run for a very long time. Most of us have done this. At a certain point we must have gotten the definite impression that if we continued running, the machine would die, and if we stopped running, we would descend into a peculiar kind of hell in which we would spend the next thirty minutes gasping for breath and making ourselves pace back and forth so the heart could recover its normal balance.

At this point we made one of two possible decisions—either we continued past this stage, at our definite risk, or returned to the sedentary state. We knew that if we persisted, there was a distinct possibility that the machine might have dropped dead. Perhaps we were right not to push the machine too far.

However, if we had the courage or stupidity to push on further, it seemed to us as if we had broken through an invisible barrier to a new, higher dimension; we may actually have felt that we could circle the entire globe with hundred-mile leaps and bounds.

This parable is only offered as an example; long-distance running is not recommended, and is definitely not representational of the state of the awakened machine.

It is just a way of comparing two definitely distinct states of

71

the machine. Actually, if we compare the second wind of running state with the state we experienced in glimpses of real awakening, we will see very quickly that the state of physical exhilaration places the machine even further in sleep.

The states between sleep and waking are not at all calm. Some of them are quite painful and we must learn to endure certain types of pain without inflicting it upon ourselves or being stupid about it. We must learn to endure the severe sensations of the awakening machine, knowing that it leads to the eventual cessation of pain.

We must not allow our foolish mental apparatuses to develop the idea that this indicates that we are expected to pull out our toenails, disfigure ourselves, or slice the arm with a razor blade, or any other foolish or bizarre practice. We must understand the differentiation between tolerating pain which occurs in the course of events and deliberately inflicting pain upon oneself unnecessarily and foolishly.

There have arisen a number of methods which utilize exhaustion, physical, mental and emotional, as a means of carrying the machine across the threshold from the sleeping state to the waking state.

It is true that the machine can be forced into awakening by the use of certain very strenuous exercises, but these methods are only for the use of people who are desperately in a hurry because of serious illness or because of pending death, who have no time to use gentler and more permanent awakening methods.

Every real school has a variety of methods, some very cathartic, some very gentle, running the entire range intended for different pupils with different needs. The cathartic methods are reserved only for those in dire, desperate need, because under ordinary conditions they are unnecessarily dangerous and life-threatening. Some of the cathartic methods represent very real threats to mental health, to emotional stability.

Very rapid methods of awakening the machine do exist, but their percentage of casualties and failures is very high. Between the casualties and the failures, the chance of success in these methods is far too small.

A very popular school existing today is founded on the principles of just such a cathartic method. Its founder must have attended a school for a short time and accidentally discovered or overheard one method for awakening the machine usually reserved for cases of dire emergency.

He evidently thought that one single technique would make a marvelous method, so he quickly left the work community and founded his own community, where he applied this technique, which he called the fast path, to everyone who came, obviously thinking that it would be just wonderful for everyone to wake up their machines really in a hurry by next Saturday at the very latest.

He did not understand that cathartic techniques are reserved as a tool only for the desperate, for those who have a very short time remaining to them in the machine, and who are forced to work quickly in a desperate race against time.

Ordinarily our system is noncathartic and extremely mild, developing the will of the essential self gently, and awakening the machine slowly, so that it does not go too far out of balance.

At the same time, because we use a noncathartic method, we can begin to study the Work while the machine is in a waking state. It is only in the waking state that the Work can be studied. We will discuss this in detail at a later time.

In addition to its two objective states of waking and sleeping, the machine also has a variety of subjective states.

As we gather evidence to convince ourselves once and for all to our own satisfaction that the machine is asleep, some of our evidence will be found by the observation of the machine's subjective states.

When the machine is awake it does not and cannot have subjective states because all the machinery for subjective states is gone. In our glimpses of the awakened state, we may have noticed the absence of subjective states.

Of course, because the machine was not completely awake, some vestigial traces of the machine's ordinary states would have remained, but unless we give them force, they cannot produce an imbalance which would send us down into the sleeping state once again.

In our early experiments with the waking state, we will undoubtedly notice the presence of phantom thoughts, phantom beliefs, and phantom attitudes, but we should easily recognize them as phantom, nonreal...something generated by the intellectual or emotional functions of the mental centrum, a leftover from the sleeping state.

If these did happen to have noticeable force, then we would have been driven by them, by what is called in some traditions, the wind of karma. These phantom reverberations of organic habits of the machine may tend to remain with us for quite some time, long after we have extricated ourselves from the machine, and if we do not deal with them now by repeated awakenings, they will tend to persist long after the end of our organic sojourn in the life of the machine.

The first objective aim is to gather evidence of the machine's sleep. We can do this now, as we are, even in sleep. As a matter of fact, if we think about it, it is only in sleep that we can gather evidence of the machine's sleep.

This is an accomplishable aim. All we need for the gathering of evidence of the machine's sleep is a minimum of attention; we don't even need the help of any supernatural agency like the mysterious "soul" or some other ethereal observer.

All we really need is sufficient ordinary attention of the mental apparatus to gather enough good evidence to satisfy ourselves that we do in fact live in a human biological machine and that, in relation to another, much higher state, it is asleep.

As we first begin, because we turn our attention on the machine, naturally we won't find the machine sleeping. It will awaken partially because it is under the awakening spotlight of attention. Unfortunately, this is one of the biggest problems about the observation of the machine.

When we observe the machine, it awakens slightly, enough so that we cannot really say that it is asleep.

Direct observation of the machine has the effect of changing the thing that is being observed. It is a broad application of the Heisenberg Principle.

If we cannot gather evidence of the machine's sleep by direct observation of its sleep, we can gather a different kind of evidence by comparing its present state to the state in which we remember the machine was at least partially awake, and we can say that it is not that way.

We gather this direct evidence by contrasting our present experience of perceptions, senses, sensations and knowledge against the background of those expanded perceptions, sharpened and magnified senses, tingling sensations of real, living tissue, and vast all-encompassing knowledge which we remember vividly from the partially awakened state.

Even if we have never experienced a single glimpse of the awakened state, we need not proceed just on faith alone; even without a direct experience of the awakened state, we can compile more than sufficient indirect evidence of sleep to convince any judge and jury that the machine is asleep beyond a shadow of a doubt.

Indirect evidence is comprised of two types of evidence, the first of which we will call "circumstantial evidence". We suddenly find ourselves slightly awake, having popped out of our total sleep for the moment. Because we are no longer entirely immersed in sleep, we cannot observe the sleep of the machine directly.

We know that what a sleeping machine does when it is asleep can only be compiled after the fact. We may be startled awake, only to realize that the machine has exerted its will over the situation.

We may see a variety of additional symptoms of sleep. Sleep presents in many different ways. In sleep, the machine exerts its own will and we have no voice in its behavior; our higher aims are lost in the organic storms of the machine as it follows one organic distraction and attraction after another.

We are carried along helplessly by the machine in its mechanical pursuits.

Another symptom of the sleep of the machine is that we find ourselves for some inexplicable reason actually following what we know to be trivial aims.

We find ourselves protecting property, trying to enhance our personal behavior and appearance. To our utter amazement we find ourselves really caring about the kind of car we drive or the quality of manufacture of our Italian shoes and fourteen-karat gold chains, or whether or not we look good in sunglasses.

We suddenly discover that we care what people think about us and we really are concerned about which politician gets into office. We find ourselves immersed in the excitement of a Tupperware plastic food-storage container sales party, and in a frenzy over exactly which Tupperware set we should buy. And if not Tupperware, then the new miracle Cambridge weight-loss diet powder or the new French Moulinex food-processor.

If we happen to observe the machine during the event, the machine will awaken slightly, and no longer exert its will. It will behave quite differently. We must not try to stop the machine from its activities in sleep before we have gathered all the evidence we need that the machine is asleep.

In the beginning we must not exert any effort to awaken the machine. We must be quite clear on this fact.

But we can look back on the machine's behavior and activities over the past several minutes, hours or days, and note the patterns of behavior, fixations, moods, states, subjective states, pursuits of the machine, interests of the machine, and the exertion of the will of the machine over the situation.

This should give us more than sufficient circumstantial

evidence that, although the machine is not completely asleep just now, it definitely was asleep until we happened to snap out of it just enough to be able to make our observation.

This type of evidence is indirect because we became aware of the sleeping state only after the fact; we look back at the previous state of the machine. Even though vestiges of the sleeping state remain, we can never truly observe the machine in sleep, *because all observation awakens the machine slightly*.

The best evidence of the machine's sleep will not be gathered by ourselves; it will be gathered by others who make their observations of our machine while it is in sleep. We will call this "hearsay evidence".

We can use this type of observation from the platform of an outside observer to gather very exact data about the sleep of our machine, insofar as it is observable from outside.

We will gather evidence of the machine's sleep for thirty days exactly, keeping precise records in special notebooks labeled "Exhibit A", to mean direct evidence, "Exhibit B", to indicate circumstantial evidence and "Exhibit C", to denote hearsay evidence, using as many notebooks as necessary over the observation period.

All evidence must be clearly indicated as *direct*, *circumstantial*, and *hearsay*.

Because our machines are asleep, we cannot trust them to help us remember to make these observations every day without fail, so we are forced to rely upon an age-old salesman's trick; we will set a time limit for ourselves.

We must agree to make these observations for a full thirty

days, *but no more*. This is a once-in-a-lifetime effort. If we are to gather the force for observation in sufficient potency, we must agree that no matter what happens, after the thirty-day observation period, we will never again make this effort.

If we recall the last glimpse of the awakening of the machine that we had, we may realize to our shock that it wasn't all that recent, and it is because these momentary glimpses are so far apart that we are able to gather so much evidence so quickly that the machine is asleep most of the time, and even when it isn't, it might as well be, because it clings to the vestiges of the sleeping state even during the waking state.

E.J. Gold, Inside Outside , Charcoal on Arches 1987

CHAPTER 10

The Machine as an Electrical Field

The human biological machine is a powerful dominant electrical field which can, if its transformational functions are activated by the waking state, act electrically upon the essential self . . . another, less powerful but more subtle electrical field which forms the true self.

Hundreds of years ago, before the time of Luigi Galvani, a professor of anatomy at Bologna University in Italy, very little was known about the human biological machine, and it was a long time before anyone thought to apply Galvani's experiments with muscular electricity to the idea that a human being is an electrical field within a larger electrical field which we call biological life.

Galvani had been dissecting some frogs. He happened to touch the disconnected leg of one frog with two different metals, producing a slight electrical current in the leg. He was

81

astounded to see the leg twitch and contract in muscular spasms, in spite of the fact that the leg had been entirely severed from the frog's body.

Galvani became convinced that electricity was the driving force behind the motor functions and nervous system and brain of the body; that animal electricity was the life-force itself.

This idea was popularized by Mary Wollstonecraft Shelley in her romantic novel, "Frankenstein".

Here is the basis for the modern discoveries by science that the human machine is a storage capacitor for, and directed by, electricity, and that the brain is a condenser filled with latent electrical energy, ready at any moment to charge any nerve, setting its corresponding muscle into contraction.

We can use this in an entirely different way, if we only know the exact mental and emotional keys to activate in order to produce the reflex reaction we want from the machine.

Now scientists all over the world are beginning to prove that what ancient schools taught, that the human being is essentially an electrical field, is literally true.

Schools have long taught that the human being under ordinary conditions, living with ordinary habits of life, is only partially able to generate this electrical force, but that the human biological machine can quickly be transformed into a powerful living dynamo, capable of generating enormous units of electrical force, vibrating with this pure life-force in every nerve and muscle fibre.

This living electrical dynamo which has been verified by science, is only a small part of the evolutionary process, yet this secret, drawn from ancient teachings which have remained hidden for tens of centuries from the mainstream of human life, can be used to build up the human biological machine's storage of vital energy.

Eventually we inevitably discover that true mastery of the self is mastery of the electrical field of which the self is composed.

Not only are most human beings unable to function as a living electrical dynamo; they are running on dead batteries, because their electrical force is dissipated by nervous fidgeting, agitation, worry, wrong foods, ragged breathing, melancholy, deep irritability, emotional upheavals and other destructive habits of the machine.

Electricity is stored in the nerve centers and brain masses, but it is easily possible to increase the potential of these energies simply by eliminating these bad habits and then awakening the machine.

The machine's function as a machine is both electrical and chemical. For instance, when the machine is startled, frightened or upset, adrenalin is automatically released, and immediately we sense definite chemical and electrical changes.

One such change is that the skin sweats, adding saltwater to the surface, which reduces the resistance of the skin, as anyone who has a background in basic physics knows.

A current passes more quickly through saltwater and the presence of a saltwater solution on the skin makes it a better conductor.

The moving centrum in the tailbrain directs a signal to those muscles in the particular part of the body it wishes to move, and those muscles contract to the degree corresponding to the electrical force which enters the muscle.

We can test this pure galvanic response by applying an electrical current to a dead muscle. The muscle will accordingly undergo contraction and relaxation with the application and removal of the electrical current.

Much of our ordinary muscle tension is the result of an overabundance of electrical force in the muscle. The tissue becomes tense as electrical resistance builds up.

The muscle builds a charge and is unable to release it. We say that electrical force has packed up in the muscle.

At some point this electrical force would build up and then be released spasmodically. The muscle acts as a capacitor under microvoltage and microamperage.

Think of the human biological machine as a transformational apparatus which, because it is a powerful dominant electrical field, can—if it is properly activated, by which we mean awake—act electrically upon the essential self, which is another, less powerful but more subtle electrical field.

Under the influence of the awakened human biological machine, the essential self will undergo a series of transformations which are electrical in nature.

Very minute electrical changes occur in the machine in microvolts and microamperes of current. Almost all this electrical activity is in the four to twenty-eight Hertz, or cycles-per-second frequency spectrum.

Some electrical fields are very destructive to the subtle electrical activity of the machine, and we must take this into account if we expect it to operate as a transformational apparatus.

The whole planet is permeated with electro-magnetic waves generated by various electrical transmission devices, for example, the normal commercial electrical current alternating at sixty cycles per second.

These currents pass through the atmosphere and are destructive to transformational efforts. Our work must take into account the effect of a variety of transmitted frequencies ranging from standard waves to microwaves coming from a variety of electrical sources such as radios, electrical appliances, power lines, automobiles, telephone lines; anywhere we have a flow of electricity, we also have its corresponding electro-magnetic wave, and both the machine and the essential self are affected by this, particularly by wires which carry electrical energy.

The flow of electricity in a wire creates a relatively tremendous electrical field along its axis, setting up a new pattern in the field surrounding it such as appears on a computer disc when placing a paper clip upon it, producing an electrical anomaly, a local variation in the field caused by the appearance of a new, smaller electrical field within the body of the larger electrical field.

A radio station operating in the Russian city of Minsk sends radio waves through the atmosphere, which reach us not only through electrical changes in the atmosphere, but through the earth itself, by making slight alterations in the magnetic structure of the earth.

Although we cannot register the reception of these atmospheric electrical anomalies in the form of radio signals amplified in our bodies, nevertheless the combined effect of all transmitted electrical signals, echoes, skips and bounces which are only some of the atmospheric phenomena of radio waves passing through us at any given moment causes an unending series of profound topological distortions in the body's local electrical field.

Radio waves, x-rays, ultraviolet radiation, high-frequency transmissions and very low frequency transmissions such as those used between submarines and their home bases, and many other artificial radiations produced by human ingenuity, radically alter the whole electrical field of force of the Earth from moment to moment, twenty-four hours a day.

The earth is a giant magnet and wherever we find a magnet, we also find electricity. Wherever we find gravity, we find electricity and magnetism.

Microchanges in the body can alter not just the body's health, but its higher function as a transformational apparatus.

E.J. Gold, Questions, Questions, Charcoal on Sennelier, 1989

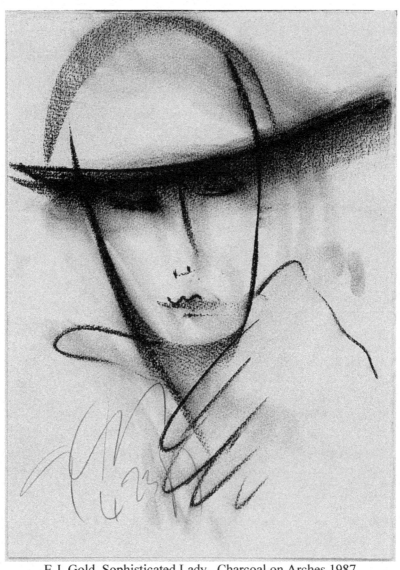

E.J. Gold, Sophisticated Lady , Charcoal on Arches 1987

CHAPTER 11

The Repair of the Machine

Because life experiences—mnemonically stored in the muscles of the body—have distorted the electrical field of the machine, repair of these anomalies in the general electrical field are necessary in order for the machine to function effectively as a transformational apparatus.

The machine stores all its memory electromagnetically, and releases it according to electrochemically transmitted instructions.

The entire headbrain corresponds to the information handling part of a computer, called the processor, and the data-storage units are represented by the muscles; the buss lines which strap across the whole system, providing a common referent-base to which the oppositely charged voltage variations representing information encapsulated within an electrical carrier wave of raw electrical voltage refer, is represented by the central nervous system; and the data-retrieval mechanism is represented by the autonomic nervous system and the basebrain which calls up information by stimulation of precise portions of the myoneural network.

Take a moment to realize the implications of this. It means that the entire experiential history of the machine is stored in the smaller electrical fields of the muscles.

Each new experience tends to overlay and refer to all previous similar experiences or experiences which seem similar whether they are or not. The storage mechanism is incapable of determining the actual reliability of its estimation of similarity, and often the seeming similarity is completely false.

Experiences which seem to be the same tend to be stored in the same memory sector, although they may not necessarily be related to the same event and the similarity may not be evident when examined closely. Similarities may be based upon one element within the experience, and the element may not be actually significant.

For example, events may seem similar to the storage mechanism because they contain an object which is common to each, or a color, odor or emotion which produces the apparency of similarity.

Eventually, because these experiences are stored electrically in the muscles, the machine becomes bent with age just from the sheer weight of life-experience.

Impressions, or memory-events—events in the sense of their meaning in physics, mathematics and chemistry—are directed by the machine to various storage elements in the muscles, not necessarily as they occur, and definitely not with any ordered logic. They accumulate in the muscle system according to the machine's own internal reasoning and customary habit.

The muscles are operated by what is called myo-electrical current, conducted by the neural network which runs through the muscles.

With repeated aggravation, the muscles tend to remain more or less permanently constricted, which radically distorts the shape and function of the muscles, in turn distorting the electrical field of the machine as a whole.

Stored information distorts the muscles because the muscles store information as an electrical field whose shape represents the information. This shaped electrical field can be expressed as a geometric and algebraic mathematical function which reflects the exact informational content of the muscle.

The muscles are shot through with very small low-resistance electrical transmission lines which behave more or less like electrical wires and, just like wires, they develop electromagnetic ridges and valleys around themselves which reflect their function and which are altered by, and reciprocally alter, any adjacent electrical fields within their sphere of influence.

In this sense, the shape of an electrical storage apparatus can be said to determine its function, and the function in turn reciprocally determines the form of the electrical field as the storage apparatus accommodates itself to its contents and functions.

Automatically as an experience is recorded in the muscles, the local electrical field is correspondingly altered.

Repeated intentional stimulation and restimulation of the

brain and the myo-electrical systems tend, over a period of time, if we are exact in our method, to alter the smaller microelectrical fields of surrounding glands and muscles, which can have the effect of activating the machine as a functional transformational apparatus which performs exactly as we intend it to. We will discuss the intentional restimulation of the neural network in a later talk.

It is the neural network which controls, directs and monitors the machine in its separate functions, and the thalamus blends this information into a balanced whole; then transmitting its analysis to the reasoning centrums, which may respond with further instructions.

Unfortunately, the thalamus does not listen to reason.

Extremely localized intra- and infra-cellular current may or may not pass into the neurological network, but when they do, this also affects the general electrical field of the machine.

While the headbrain acts as the central data-processor, the muscles are the actual data storage areas and, because they generate their own micro-fields on a cellular level, they are capable of independent functioning of a relatively high order without the direction of the larger brains.

Alteration of the electrical field of the muscles alters the function of the machine as a transformational apparatus. If it is not functioning effectively even though awake, we can intentionally make alterations by stimulating specific portions of the brain and myo-electrical systems with special exercises, to repair the machine as a transformational apparatus.

Ringing out the wires of the nervous system is in the category of repairs to the machine. We must not only look at the transformation of the machine but the repair of the machine as well.

Any biological machine, if awakened, will function as a transformational apparatus, but blind transformation of the essential self by the machine doesn't mean anything specific, and even very minor variances in the machine's functioning and electrical field will alter its transformational function.

Even a crude instrument such as a galvanic skin response meter—originally called a Glame-Meter, which measures the conductivity of the skin in terms of all the machine's electrical changes, first invented in the latter half of the nineteenth century by Webster Edgerly, the founder of the Ralston Health Club, and later manufactured as a modern biofeedback apparatus during the mid- nineteen-fifties by the Mathison Meter Company in Los Angeles— can give us an accurate picture of the functioning of the machine as a transformational apparatus.

The meter, a balanced Wheatstone Bridge which compares the electrical resistance of the body on one side of the bridge to a known ballast resistance on the other side of the bridge, in much the way that a balance scale compares an unknown weight against a known weight, takes a continuous sampling of the average of all the electrical results of all the smaller electrical fields, presenting them as a logarithmic function, in contrast to which, we can see the electrical resistances represented as anomalies—displacements—in the general electrical field, as clearly as if we were able to view them photographically.

Music will serve as an example. Music can be said to be a logarithmic function in which an analog sampling of the totality of tonic notes presents itself to the ear. The analog sampling is taken at definite periodic intervals.

What we actually hear as music is the average sampling of what remains after the sound has been categorically destroyed by conflicting harmonics and overtones.

We do not hear the tonic sounds themselves. What we hear is the elimination of the tonic—the subtonic of the original sound.

After the harmonics and overtones have destroyed the tonic, we are left with all the sounds that were *not* made, the sounds left over from the original sound.

A new tonic is introduced to this average sound, and then the process begins all over again. This principle should be taught to every child before they even learn arithmetic.

A galvanic skin response meter takes rapid, almost continuous, samplings of the entire electrical field of the human biological machine, producing a reading only when an anomaly is present, a disturbance in the field of the force.

If we intentionally activate some particular sector of memory in the muscles, this will produce an electrical anomaly, which would appear instantaneously as a reading on the galvanic skin response meter.

We must understand that we are not considering the artificial alteration of function of the machine in the sense of its behavior, but the repair of the machine's dominant electrical field which has a complex influence upon the more subtle electrical field which we call the essential self, which effect can be expressed as a continuously variable complex exponential equation.

We need very little theory to be able to use this idea. For

example, we may have no idea of the theory of automotive design and engineering, but with the right information, we are capable of driving and even repairing a car.

In the same way, we need not understand the exact electrical equations which reflect the influence of one electrical field upon another in order to use the principle for the repair of the machine as a transformational apparatus.

For a complete understanding, we would need a background in Reimannian space theory, Wavicle Theory, theory of local gravitational effects, the low-energy plasma theory, the General and Special field theories—within which we will find the Law of Relativity in a very different form from its popularization—the gravitational attraction of nucleic functions and non-charged particles, functions of probability, indeterminacy, quark-quark relationships, vector analysis, energy transfer, non-Euclidian geometric functions, topological functions of complex-connected volumes, beat-frequency oscillation, electromagnetic relationships to the light and sound spectrum, and other brain-boggling mathematical concepts which relate to the impingement of two slightly dissimilar electrical fields.

But all this is unnecessary. We need only enough information to understand the basic mechanics of the repair of the machine as a transformational apparatus, not the repair of the machine as a machine regarding its physical, emotional and mental functions.

Even without a theoretical understanding, we would, with a little study, be able to see what needs repair.

The galvanic skin response meter will definitely tell us whether or not there is an electro-magnetic anomaly—an evoked reaction which indicates an electrical resistance, an impaction—upon the general electrical field.

We will notice micro-changes in the electrical field of the machine. The needle will move up and down the ohmic spectrum, from five hundred to one million ohms, within which the meter can measure even the smallest obstruction.

We can determine whether an electrical blockage was eliminated completely and permanently by the response indicated on the meter.

We can intentionally repeatedly stimulate—according to an exact sequential plan—definite portions of the brain and nervous system, thus eliminating local distortions in the electrical field which are, when they are active, measurable as electrical anomalies, having definite and tangible electrical effects and phenomena.

If the muscles are impacted with electrical barriers which are activated by the machine's defense mechanism against the waking state, then we should see a larger response of the meter. When we have eliminated the distortions in the field, we will have disarmed the defense mechanism and the machine will naturally remain in the waking state unless we intentionally produce the sleeping state for the purpose of rest and conservation of work-energies.

The content of memory itself is not important; we are only interested in the distortion it produces upon the electrical field of the essential self. We do not know where memory is stored, nor do we really care, because with the meter we are able to locate and gain access to any part of memory, not by its content and significance, but by its electrical impact, its distorting effect as an interference, a blockage, in the general electrical field of the machine.

Random memory storage implies random memory accessibility. If we know how to throw electrical anomalies—displacements—into high relief against the general background of the whole electrical field, we know all we actually need to know to repair the machine as a transformational apparatus and disarm the machine's defense mechanism against the waking state.

But we do not have time to analyze every little detail of the functioning of the machine. A complete analysis would be too time-consuming and far too complex. And the fact is that this is unnecessary. It is quicker and more efficient to repair everything in the machine's functioning as a transformational apparatus, whether it needs it or not.

In our repair work, we stimulate the brain and nervous system in very specific ways, until the anomaly, the displaced charge or blockage, disappears.

Because this electrical energy which had been stored in the muscles as resistors is now available to the machine at large, the neural network enlarges, becomes more active and activates more fully as the electrical potential increases.

At the same time, blockages in the neuro-muscular system also disappear, allowing the whole neural network to flow more freely. The entire body becomes a more effective electrical field which has an exact effect on the electrical field which we call the essential self.

Electricity in the body, which had formed into eddies and disturbances because of the distortion factors stored in the muscles and nervous system, is free to flow as it did during early childhood, before conditioning and inhibitors were imposed by life-experiences and suggestion by mimicry of others, and the original shape and condition of the electrical field of the machine is restored in general.

The electro-magnetic anomalies do not recur once they have been eliminated. Information and memory are not lost. Actually, they are enhanced because they become more accessible now that we have eliminated the painful and unwanted electrical field distortion which surrounded them.

E.J. Gold, Listen To My Shouts, Charcoal on Rives BFK, 1996

E.J. Gold, Snowden Is Odin , Charcoal on Arches 1987

CHAPTER 12

The Essential Self as an Electrical Field

Information in the evolutionary sense is transmitted by impingement of one electrical field upon another. The electrical field of the essential self undergoes the exact change necessary to free it from its compulsive electrical affinity for the human biological machine.

In our beginning work with the machine as an electrical field, we will work on the dissipation of distortions which have impacted themselves in and around the muscles.

Later on, we will disarm the data-processor in the machine itself, after which we will address the thalamus, which is a primary source for habits. We will work to clear up the machine's organic tendencies and fixations.

Then we will turn our attention to the second level,

addressing the electrical field of the essential self. At this point we use the most sensitive settings on the meter so that we can read extremely minute electrical effects and phenomena which have been exposed by the removal of the dominant electrical activity of the machine. We will discuss more about this later, in relation to the machine's tendency to impose its own will when in the sleeping state and its total lack of will in the waking state, during which the relatively weak will of the essential self becomes active in the sense that it is no longer buried under the dominating force of the machine's will.

Our ability to survive in the fourth dimension will be determined by our familiarity with it. In a zero gravity-simulator, we would experience the conditions of orbital or deep space flight.

In the waking state, we will effectively reproduce the experience of the higher dimensions; we will learn what we need to do to work and to survive in the higher dimensions.

The essential self is an electrical field and the machine generates an electrical field which impinges on the essential self's electrical field.

The crystallized electrical field of the being replaces the machine as a body of matter. The machine as matter is replaced by a steady-state electromagnetic image of itself. The crystallized electric field becomes a reflection of its own reflection.

If the machine is functioning as a transformational apparatus, then the machine as an electrical field should eventually take the form of what the essential self will someday become, at least in the electrical sense.

What can the essential self learn from the machine?

Nothing in the intellectual sense, and we must realize that learning in the electrical sense, which is called "understanding" in our tradition, means something quite different from what is ordinarily understood by the word "learning".

Information in the evolutionary sense is transmitted by impingement of one electrical field upon another. The electrical field of the essential self undergoes change—which we call "transformation", by which we mean the exact changes necessary to free it from its electrical affinity for the human biological machine within which it takes its current involuntary residence—as a result of "learning" from the electrical field of the machine.

That is, it learns from the machine's electrical field if the machine is not in the sleeping state and the field is not damaged or distorted by conditioning.

In addition, another factor is necessary if the machine is to function as a teacher to the essential self, imposing its field functions upon that of the essential self.

Even though the machine wishes, in a way, to fulfill its function as a transformational apparatus, in the same way that all living organisms "wish" to fulfill their genuine objective functions, it also has developed a powerful defense mechanism against the waking state. We will discuss this at length very soon, in relation to the practical method for bringing the machine into the waking state.

The greater the similarity of the electrical field of the machine to that of the essential self, the greater the possibility for the principle of contagion to alter the electrical field of the essential self.

Like affects like, and then eventually, like *becomes* like, indicating the exact method for the possible evolution of the essential self.

Stroke a needle with a magnet. What happens? The needle becomes slightly magnetized. Its electromagnetic field becomes slightly aligned with that of the magnet.

Repeatedly stroke the electrical field of the essential self with the electrical field of the machine and the essential self becomes aligned with the machine.

We can use the awakened machine to get our own way, make our own rules, pursue one form of trivia or another, or we can exert our will toward the awakening of the machine for our possible evolution.

We may experience a situation in which the machine's electrical blockages are temporarily removed by artificial means—drugs, hypnosis, or some sort of shock—and the machine functions momentarily as it should, as a pure, vital, living electrical apparatus.

In an experience in which the machine's electrical field is temporarily cleared artificially of its distortions, we have all the voluntariness of a passenger on a roller-coaster.

We are forced to watch ourselves helplessly as we are slammed around from one state to another, propelled through these experiences gently, but inexorably.

Accidentally or intentionally perceiving another dimension, crossing a barrier to another dimension, we might notice the loss of significance and meaning—a lack of logical coherence; and yet at the same time, we might suddenly experience the deep, living connectedness of everything—being of subject and object as much as of oneself.

Perceiving in more than one dimension at a time is very unusual: it is more usual to perceive in one dimension and then to return to another. Ordinary perception is single-dimensional.

A normally functioning human being should have the ability to perceive and function in several dimensional levels at the same time.

Perceiving in single dimensions produces the illusion of separation but if we are able to function as a multi-dimensional being, then we will view ourselves and our surroundings as miniature electrical fields, anomalies within one giant electrical field, and eventually the electrical field of the essential self will stabilize itself in the transformed state.

E.J. Gold, No Time To Stop , Charcoal on Arches 1990

CHAPTER 13

Help

Real help is not someone doing something for us, or a lessening of our personal suffering and struggles. Real help has no calming effect—quite the contrary—it makes the machine squirm itself into evolution-by-reflex.

We have such high, wonderful ideas! Such complicated and exalted psychological and philosophical explanations, such noble intentions for ourselves...

Then, all of a sudden, in spite of our best intentions and our strongest wishes, things go wrong and we sink into deep, dark negative states. From the depths of the volcano of the deep self, an explosion erupts, destroying all our noble dreams and illusions in its wake. What became of our high ideals and noble intentions?

Deep down in the darkest, most primitive levels of the machine, someone or something, the most inaccessible part of ourselves, makes it impossible for us to actually carry out our highest aims and aspirations.

The will of the machine toward self-gratification and sleep is very different from the high ideals of the essential self, which has marvelous plans.

Periodic emotional storms constantly serve as reminders that the machine has a will of its own.

The essential self, with its great ideals, is unfortunately not the director of the machine and, under ordinary circumstances, can never be the director of the machine or anything else including itself. As it is, the essential self is a slave, not a master, and yet it was made to be master.

Our biggest lie about ourselves, besides the absurd idea that man is not just another species of primate belonging to the animal kingdom on the Earth, is that the essential self is the director—the absolute autocrat—of the machine, when we can clearly see from our daily experience that it has no will over the machine whatsoever.

The machine exercises its destructive will, completely disregarding the intentions of the essential self. This conflict gives the illusion of many different identities each acting on its own.

Really, there are only two: the intelligence which formulates the higher aims and aspirations, and the primitive brain, which is the real director of the machine, because its savage will is completely dominant.

We are in the grip of the machine's private insanity, forced to live as we would never live if we were able to actually exert our will upon the machine, to control and direct its activities every moment of the day.

Yet we tell ourselves the lie that the mental apparatus is the director of the machine. Originally, the meaning of virtue was that the noble aims and aspirations of the essential self had reached down through the mental apparatus and rooted itself into the deepest part of the machine and that the aims and aspirations of the deepest darkest part of the machine had in fact become the same as those of the essential self.

In our beginning work, we first encounter the idea that we are expected to apply a method, some technique unknown to us in ordinary life, which can somehow help us to penetrate through to the deepest, darkest part of the machine and plant our ideals in it. Our ideals become an incarnate reality in flesh and blood. At last, we are one with the machine, in this sense at least.

This is a very ancient idea expressed in the majority of Greek philosophy, which was expressed at that time not just by gatherings to discuss interesting ideas, but schools of practical knowledge. We will find these same ideas in Plato's "Symposium", and in the teachings of Pythagoras.

Once we have seriously studied the machine and clearly understood the real nature of our situation, we will see that we have only three choices.

We can refuse to acknowledge our total lack of will over the machine, and pointedly ignore the inner emotional storms and external upheavals caused by the machine against all our higher intentions.

The second choice is to lower our standards, to make ideals for ourselves which conform more to the actual swinish behavior of the machine.

109

The third choice is the most difficult. We can search for a method, a practical means, by which the machine is brought to a state which actually reflects the highest ideals of our essential self in the deepest fibers of its being.

It is not necessary to bring the machine to its knees on every issue. It is only necessary to awaken the machine because only a sleeping machine exercises its will.

An awakened machine cannot possess negative force, and since negative force provides the force for the exertion of its will, an awakened machine has no will of its own. Without the force of its own will, the machine comes to a standstill. When the machine is awake, even the subtle suggestions of the essential self, which has no weapon but attention, is sufficient to direct the machine.

There is no way to fight the machine directly, to make a direct attack, and win. No method of training and drilling the machine to conform to higher aims and aspirations can remain in force throughout the life of the machine. At some point, all ordinary methods of training the machine to obedience will fail.

We can have the best intentions in the world, the best aesthetics, the most marvelous plans for ourselves, yet if the machine continues to behave monstrously, all our plans will come to nothing, all our high ideals will be useless.

We must accomplish two things. First, we must find some way to define, delineate, clarify what are our exact ideals. Then we must see that we do not have the will to bring the entire machine into action as a unified whole.

When we formulate an aim, if the machine has no will of its own, we are unified, a true republic. This inner unity of higher aspirations of the essential self and the deepest most primitive part of the machine, is the real meaning of the ideal of Utopia, the perfect republic.

I am, but more than this, *I have become*. In ancient times, the awakened machine was referred to as the "living father" because it was recognized that the machine is the father of the soul. When the machine and I reflect one another, then the machine, the father, and I are one, and the machine is a reflection of my innermost being.

When we make the outer as the inner, the inner as the outer, then I and the father—the essential self and the human biological machine—are one.

It must be clearly understood that the Work cannot be studied through a sleeping machine; the Work means nothing to a sleeping machine. A sleeping machine cares only for itself, its aims, its problems and its pursuits.

A sleeping machine is hypnotized by its own subjective fixations and beyond those fixations there is no objective reality.

It is deaf and blind to the Work and even to higher ideals, because it is asleep. The Work cannot be defined because it is living, growing, and changing. The word "living" was once the same as the word "awake".

The essential self has no will, except the will-of-attention. It can place its attention on something, it can direct its attention. By bathing the machine in its attention, it awakens the machine.

The force of the attention of the essential self is slow and subtle, like the tortoise. The machine's attention is like the rabbit, rapidly darting this way and that, distracted by every little thing, convinced of its own innate superiority. This is the idea behind the ancient myth of the tortoise and the hare.

The subtle force of attention is our only weapon against sleep. It is a very effective weapon if we are able to see that because it is subtle, it must be applied unremittingly, unwaveringly, over a very long period of time.

If someone else uses the force of attention to wake up our machine, the will of our own essential self will not develop. An awakened machine is not enough. We also want to develop the will of the essential self so that when the machine is awake, and its will has vaporized, we are able to exert our will toward our possible evolution.

If we refuse work, we refuse help. Work *is* help. If we want real help, and not our imaginary ideas of what help is, we must accept it in the form it comes, not in the form we expect. Real help is not someone doing something for us, or a lessening of our personal struggles.

The sleeping machine cannot recognize help. Help makes the enemy squirm; if the enemy does not squirm, then it is not real help.

It is important to recognize the consequences of asking for real help; if we want calming, we should ask for calming. If we want *real help* we must ask for real help, and understand it when it is given. We may not like the results, but real results will make the machine squirm—no pain, no gain.

We must develop a definite courage to ask for help because we may actually get what we ask for. Humility is also necessary; we must be able to recognize that we are not capable of helping ourselves.

Then in addition, we must have the stamina, the fortitude, to survive the help.

Purity and virtue help us place ourselves in a situation in which help can be given. What virtue really means is that the mind and the machine are one, in the sense that what the mind conceives, the machine achieves.

E.J. Gold, In a Mirror Darkly, Charcoal on Arches 1996

CHAPTER 14

Alchemy

Alchemy is not a way of producing behavioral change in the machine; it is a way of notating change that occurs on a much deeper level. It is not a cause, but an effect, a reflection of the inner evolution of the essential self.

We normally think that we have our whole lives to accomplish this work, but the fact is that our energy for transformation will have dissipated itself by the time we are older.

We must have completed the transformational process before we run out of the resilience and flexibility required to complete the alchemical process of transformation.

Alchemy is a discipline in which an individual uses the machine to refine different substances, combining and separating and processing them by various means, over a long period of time, through the use of slow heat—by which is meant the application of inexorable and unwavering attention —producing a chemical and electrical mutation of the machine which is only a reflection of a much deeper internal mutation of the essential self.

With ordinary methods, we can learn chemistry, a very simple subject, wherein we pour a chemical substance from one beaker to another. It is easy to see and measure our results because the process is all external.

In the process of alchemy, however, we are dealing with the chemical factory hidden within the human biological machine.

In this case, we cannot just pour from one beaker to another. To obtain exact results, we must stimulate by very precise means definite sectors of the brain and nervous system, which in turn stimulate muscle and nervous system interactions, releasing chemicals through the use of heat and electricity, causing substantive changes in the machine.

We are not dealing with beakers and test tubes, but with very minute chemical changes which are governed by the glandular system, brain and nervous system. If we know exactly how to stimulate the brain and nervous system, it will in turn stimulate the glandular system, muscular system, and vascular system, stimulating and retarding chemical changes.

This process of alternate stimulation and retardation was called in the Western alchemical tradition "solve et coagula".

Because we are stimulating the brain and nervous system, and not just pouring from one beaker to another, we are forced to use psychological and emotional methods to stimulate the brain and nervous system, which in turn will stimulate the glandular system in an exact way, producing the exact changes we wish to produce.

116

Suppose that we know exactly what it is we want to do. Suppose we know, in other words, a method, an exact strategy for change.

If we were ordinary in our approach and we followed some cookbook or other, we would psychologically stimulate thoughts and emotions which would in turn stimulate and retard chemical and electrical processes in the machine.

We are supposing in this case that the deeper internal transmutation is a product of the machine's change, but the fact is that we do not wish to change the machine directly at all; we wish to use changes in the machine as a roadmap, by which we can follow a much deeper inner change.

Alchemy is not a way of producing change in the machine; it is a way of notating change as it occurs.

If we were to follow the indications of alchemy, trying to artificially produce alchemical results directly in the machine, without the deeper internal change of which they are only a reflection, we would not see real results; just changing the temperature of the thermometer does not change the temperature of the body.

Real alchemy is not a cause, but an effect, a reflection of a change in the essential self.

An alchemical notebook is a traveler's record, a log book, a map, noting the change which has been brought about in the machine by a deeper internal mutation. In this way, the human biological machine can be utilized both as a transformational apparatus and as a biofeedback device indicating transformational changes as they occur by noting their effects upon the machine.

All the apparent complexity of alchemy disappears when we realize that all of the alchemical notations are results, not causes, of real changes in the essential self, which occur in a cumulative sequence.

So the alchemical sequence notated in alchemical notebooks is a roadmap of the evolution of the essential self.

When an alchemical event occurs in the machine, we can check it against our roadmap to see our progress and determine our next step according to our work-strategy.

And we can be sure that this change in the essential self has occurred unless we have acted directly upon the machine to produce this change artificially just for our personal enhancement.

It is possible to artificially produce what are alchemical changes in the machine without the cause, what is called the First Cause or the First Water. The First Cause is the deep change occurring in the essential self.

The catalyst *is* the machine which produces transformation in the essential self, which is then reflected in the machine which is then capable of additional transformational effects upon the essential self, provided the machine is awake to exert these transformational effects, which are reflected by the transformed essential self upon the machine.

The human biological machine then becomes a different transformational apparatus producing a different change in essential self which is reflected in the machine, which produces a further change in the machine, and because it is a different machine produces a different transformational effect, and so forth.

118

It is changing because it reflects the cumulative transformations of the essential self, becoming a different machine producing a different change which is reflected in the machine producing a different change reflecting the machine in an upward spiral of mutual reciprocal initiation. Once this process begins, there is no stopping it.

If the machine falls asleep, the process does not stop, *it simply ceases to continue.*

The alchemical process is cumulative. It does not regress, but it may not continue for a hundred-thousand years.

At each complete alchemical process, the process is stabilized. There is no reversal so, once begun, it must be finished, otherwise we will be forced to live in pain; the cup will not pass from us.

But this is just a temporary—in the larger scale of evolution —cessation of the process of continuation, but it is not an end, not a stop, not an escape. There is no escape. We are not a stranger here. We did not come here from a different planet.

An alchemical notebook is not a cookbook; it is a map. Can we see the difference between a cookbook and a map? A cookbook we would follow like a recipe, working backwards.

One is linear, one is not linear. The cookbook we follow step-by-step, with a map, we can look anywhere we want.

What do we actually need to know about alchemy? Awakening of the machine produces transformation, and transformation is reflected in alchemical results in the machine.

If we know how to read the map sufficiently to find the little red arrow that says, "you are here", and we know how to move this little red arrow when appropriate, in other words, we recognize changes in the machine when they occur, by having some attention on the machine, then we know everything necessary about alchemy except the details of the map, which anyone can learn just in the course of working to awaken the machine.

E.J. Gold, Out In The Cold, Charcoal on Rives BFK, 1996

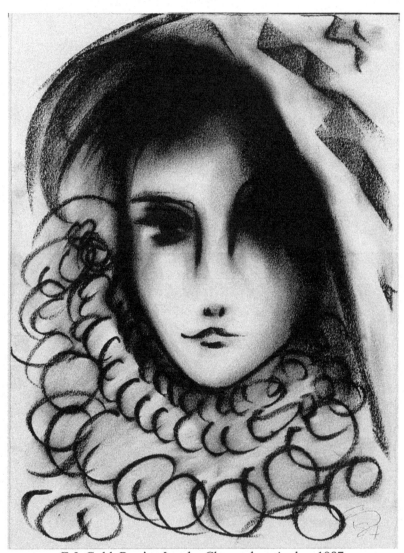

E.J. Gold, Persian Lamb , Charcoal on Arches 1987

CHAPTER 15

Bringing the Woman to Life

If we follow the machine as a lover would, unrelentingly fixing his gaze upon his Beloved, filled with astonishment, rapture and gratitude, the machine will come to life, awakening and responding to the power of adoration with a profound emotion which will in turn bring about our own transformation.

We have already established that in order for the human biological machine to be operational as a transformational apparatus, it must be in the waking state, and that only in the waking state can this function be fully activated.

How can we intentionally bring about the waking state whenever we wish to and, at the same time, know definitely that we have actually accomplished this?

Let us begin by considering the relationship of the machine and the essential self as a work partnership. What are the conditions of this partnership?

Perhaps a parallel with human relationships could help us in this matter, since in them, we can observe a similar process.

If we look at the relationship of a man and a woman and ask ourselves what it is that a woman really wants from a man, the answer is quite evident.

A woman wants a man's complete, utter, totally non-wandering attention to be placed entirely upon herself. She wants to bathe in it, to immerse herself in it, and when she is able to receive this from a man, she in turn responds with adoration.

She does not really want anything else from him, and everything she does—from cosmetics and having babies to going with him as a sailor on a barefoot cruise or sitting grimly under a blanket at a homecoming football game—serves this aim. She will do anything necessary to obtain this attention, and the more deeply profound the attention, the more centered on herself it is, the better.

Why else do you suppose that she invests many hours during the majority of her youth learning a variety of exotic walks and postures which she feels will make her seem unique and interesting?

Why does she spend hours before the mirror training her machine to smile, to laugh, to frown, to talk in a variety of tones expressing a large repertoire of moods?

Why does she learn to theatrically manipulate her mouth and eyes?

Why does she cover her face and body with scrubs, mudpacks and cosmetics, endure chemical treatments in her hair, spend hours under a hair-dryer, invest hour after hour removing body hair, giving herself a manicure, pedicure, curling her eyelashes and arranging her coiffure?

The life of an actress is not natural to her, but she knows that by these artifices she will almost certainly be able to attract and absorb the attention of a man, at least temporarily while she still has whatever it was that netted his roving attention, and she knows that he will still respond to her even if he happens to realize intellectually that she has artificially produced the glitter and flash which has happened to catch his eye and keep his attention riveted for the moment. And if this is what a woman really wants, what does a man want?

He wants his attention to be free to wander wherever it will go. He wants to be distracted and amused. His attention is scattered and fickle. It is almost as if the two genders were entirely different species, each the opposite of the other.

In order to anticipate the many directions his wandering attention will take, a woman will accommodate herself to his interests as they suddenly change tack and direction.

If he is interested in computers, she will unaccountably develop an interest in them even if she had never been interested in them before. If he is interested in sciences, she, too, will find some way to be interested and to be useful to him so that she can appear in his field of attention as he pursues his momentary fascination.

A woman who is really a woman wants this attention, and she will do absolutely anything, no matter how degrading or debased or self-effacing to her own interests, to gather the scattered attention of her man and draw it to herself. Of course she may eventually give up entirely and pursue her own interests if she is unable to obtain this attention from a man by these artifices.

But if she has any success at all in this game, she will remain interested in one thing and one thing only: a complete, deep relationship. She wants to be reached, to be touched, *to be fulfilled.*

Fulfillment is a very weak word which cannot really express the intense anguish which characterizes a woman's experience in her relationships with men, and words alone cannot do justice to the deep feelings of incompleteness and disappointment that haunt her.

With the deepest part of herself, with all her heart, she wishes to be found and *to be known.*

And so every woman has learned to become yet another glittering attraction, hoping that a man's attention will someday fall upon her, even if only accidentally—and finally come to rest upon her, warming her heart and bathing her in the intense radiation of total adoration.

It rarely happens that a man gets the message, and many women, though gifted and intelligent, have felt it necessary to resort to various forms of personal fascination in order to win —or steal—the attention of a man. Fascination seemed to be their last recourse.

To fascinate means not only to put under a spell, to charm, to captivate, but also to hold motionless, to hold someone's attention by being very interesting or delightful, or even annoying, bitchy, argumentative or congenitally ill. Anything that compels the attention can be a method, and when everything seductive fails, then nothing remains but the sad, plaintive and bitter mechanisms of neurosis, psychosomatic illness and little personal tragedies which are the common weapon of the contemporary housewife. Seductive or nagging, both mechanisms serve the same function.

A woman knows instinctively that her life can be completed through a man, but she may be unaware that this can never be achieved through an ordinary relationship with a man.

She knows that something unusual must somehow occur, but just what this may be escapes her, and her search among men in ordinary life is doomed to end in failure.

She does not know how to get his real attention, but without the Work, *even if she were able to obtain and hold his attention, she would not really know what to do with it.*

She does not know, and in the ordinary course of life cannot know, *that what she wants from a man can only be obtained through the process of mutual initiation and transformation.*

A man is in general even more ignorant than she is about this, because his interests lie completely outside the domain of deep relationships. All he knows is that he wants a new toy, and then, when he finally obtains it, he quickly tires of it and no longer wants that toy...then he wants another new toy, and yet another.

As long as his attention continues its incessant, restless wandering, he can never be initiated.

How are these two unrelated but mutually reciprocal species to be brought together?

Shall the woman say to the man: **Put your full attention on me. This is how you can accomplish what you are after.**

I know what you are after. Be with me, be fully with me, *don't take your attention away from me for a single moment.*

Thread your way through my labyrinth of love and find me. If you find me you will find what you are after, what you have been after all your life.

Were a woman to actually say this to a man, his body would make a hole in the wall exactly corresponding to its momentary shape as it hurtled through, because he could not open the door quickly enough!

How can a woman convince a man that by this mutual reciprocal initiation, something genuine can be achieved; that initiation is not out there somewhere, that it is not even deep within himself, *that it is within her?*

This has been the dilemma of women for tens of thousands of years, how to communicate to a man what a woman so deeply intuits about the process of mutual initiation, without causing his fragile ego to hopelessly fragment.

Yet a woman is willing to sit and wait very patiently for years for a man to develop from the state of restless activity, chatter and excitement, to a state of calm where he is able to just sit and be with her, where his attention stops its restless wandering and falls completely and utterly upon her.

A man can become, if he is willing to make the sacrifice, a special type of alchemical fuel to be consumed in the warming of a woman's womb, her heart of initiation, and in the process of his annihilation he is totally consumed, annihilated, as the woman comes to life.

Only when she comes to life is she able to resurrect him. Like Osiris, he must trust in his Isis, offering himself up

128

unselfishly as fuel for her inner fire, completely and without hesitation, without the slightest consideration for himself, in the same way that a mother will sacrifice herself for the sake of her children.

A man must learn from a woman that intense heart-bursting adoration which makes a woman want to devote herself to a man without concern for herself.

A woman knows how to place all of her attention on a man. She instinctively knows how to follow his moods and dispositions. She is always there, always with him. She knows what he needs. She knows what he feels. She knows his heart more than he himself does.

She has learnt to read him like a book. She knows his movements, his postures, his voice, his intonations and facial expressions, his breathing.

Even the smallest detail reveals something to her, and she is able to follow it and be there with him.

A man, on the other hand, is usually totally oblivious to a woman's changes. He does not see and cannot sense her inner moods and outer movements; he does not know how to follow her, how to read her, and in any case he does not care to; it is his opinion that she should follow him, and not he her.

But if he wishes to be initiated, he must in all things follow her. If she blinks, he must blink. If she is happy, he must be happy also. If she is sad, he too should be sad. As her moods melt one into another, he must go where she goes, and do as she does, not lagging behind but always simultaneously.

He must lose his breath, his heart, his mind to her, cleave to her, follow her, be one with her; move as one, breathe as one, think as one, feel as one, sense as one, as she does instinctively. He must learn the woman's most basic secret —"wheresoever thou goest, there also will I go".

So long as a man chooses the imaginary outer freedoms, he is choosing the life of cattle, doomed to wander from one glittering attraction to another. If only a man could use his full attention...give himself as a woman knows how to give herself!

In essence, for a man to achieve what he really wants to achieve, he must learn from a woman to be a woman and, at the same time, maintain his sanity as he loses his gender-identification and discovers what a woman really is.

If a woman hopes to accomplish her own fulfillment, she must find a real man who is willing to penetrate these deep inner secrets of a woman in order to attain the real depth of a relationship. Such a man is called an *alchemist*.

Pity a woman; she cannot tell what she knows; to protect his fragile vanity, she must appear passive, she must wait, she must be very cautious. She must not frighten her man.

She can only reveal herself when he actually has found his way through the labyrinth and arrives at her chamber. By this time, he will have lost much of what he imagined himself to be as a man; the fire will have burned away his gender pride, and he will be able to confront himself and her as two sides of the same coin. This is the true journey that beckons.

Now, in the same way, if we could view the human biological machine as a woman, as our initiator, our true teacher, and we could effectively place our restless, wandering attention completely upon it, the machine would come to life, just as a woman comes to life when a man's attention is placed upon her, completely, absolutely, unwaveringly.

The essential self is uneducated. If left to itself, it will remain passive and do nothing. It will just continue to exist, patiently waiting things out.

The machine provides the motivation for work. It understands the necessity for work. In spite of its will to remain asleep, it also yearns to serve a higher purpose.

We may be surprised to discover that it is actually the machine which seeks a school. The essential self is too detached, too complacent, for such concerns.

The machine behaves oddly in ordinary life. As we study its patterns of behavior, we discover that these peculiarities are signs of anger and frustration.

It falls into the pursuit of trivia because we rarely allow it to perform its objective function.

As these transformations take place, the machine will also undergo a series of changes. But these changes are not artificial interferences in the machine's behavior or conditioning. We must not alter this for fear of reversing the transformational process.

If we tamper even slightly with the machine, we may destroy its properties and capabilities as a transformational apparatus. In our observation of the machine, we must not be judgmental or critical; we must strive to achieve impartiality and detachment.

We are not working to change the machine. It must not change artificially if we expect to benefit from its transformational potential. We must realize that in changing the machine directly, we would unknowingly alter the very factors which make transformation possible.

This is exactly the opposite of personal enhancement methods.

As we begin our work, the relation existing between the essential self and the machine is somewhat remote and strained.

The only will that we can actually exert over the machine is the will of attention, but this will is weak and so we are continually seduced into identification with the sleep of the machine.

In the course of ordinary life, we learn to want attention but not to give it. We make basic assumptions about ourselves, which eventually become hardened beliefs. If the machine does not conform to our beliefs about ourselves, we lie to ourselves by reducing our attention on the machine still further.

Our time is limited, we have only so much time at our disposal, we don't have all our lives. Before transformation begins, we must use our attention to study the process of transformation and the methods of awakening the machine.

In addition, we must study methods of using attention to awaken the machine, methods of the unremitting placement of attention, and then somehow develop the will to actually place the attention on the machine.

We do not ordinarily have the will to place our attention unremittingly on the machine. A certain intensity of attention is required to arrive at any results whatsoever.

To obtain this intensity of attention, we must provide ourselves with an outside source of force; we can borrow the will to place our full attention on the machine by adding something to it.

This additional force which gives us the extra will necessary to fixate our attention on the machine is called *adoration*.

Adoration is an emotional ingredient, but not the emotion of the machine. It is a higher emotion which can be aroused in the essential self.

This implies, however, that the emotional centrum is fully functional, not the caricature we usually take to be our true emotional centrum, not machine reverberations emanating from the mental centrum.

In other words, before we can bring the machine to life, we must have brought to life the one centrum which is ordinarily dead in every human being, the feeling centrum.

We assume that the essential self, because it is spiritual, is endowed with special higher powers, that it is capable of many wondrous things. But the fact is, the essential self, in its present state, is quite limited. It has only two characteristics: presence and the ability to place and fixate its attention.

If we can bring the attention to stop its restless wandering, and at the same time overcome our own complacency about our situation in relation to our possible evolution, we could learn to use the machine as a transformational apparatus.

By intentionally placing our unwavering attention directly upon the machine, and following its every motion with the emotional intensity of adoration, we develop a deep relationship with the machine.

We must learn to lovingly observe not only the obvious

motor-centrum activities of the machine, but also its moods, thoughts, preferences, and attitudes, its qualities and weaknesses, what we pride ourselves on, and what we prefer to disregard.

How can we really observe the machine under our fixed gaze of unwavering attention if we do not love what we are observing? How will we even remember to hold the machine in our full attention if we are not transfixed by the machine; filled with gratitude toward its every movement, filled with astonishment and rapture?

We must follow the machine as a lover unrelentingly fixes his gaze upon his Beloved, root our attention wholly upon the machine and not let it drift. We must clearly obtain glimpses of that part of the machine which is lazy and unwilling to work, and gradually separate ourselves from it, work our way out from under its influence.

If we understand how the adoration of the woman brings her to life, then we understand how to use adoration to focus our attention upon the machine and bring it to life in the same way.

Simple attention is mental, but adoration is a function of the essential self. Adoration is much more potent.

Obviously, when we speak of adoration of the machine, we are not referring to something romantic and stupid. We intend to envelop the machine in the same intense mood of adoration which we would naturally feel toward a lover in the ordinary sense.

In certain schools, demonstrations intended as analogies to the wind-and-water technique of awakening the machine— which is to say, the inexorable pressure of unremitting attention upon the machine—are sometimes given to pupils.

Some of these demonstrations have had the unfortunate destiny of being distorted and alienated from their original meaning and purpose, and no longer serve their proper function as is so often the case with teaching tools, methods, and ideas.

One such tool is a bell used in Tibetan Buddhist schools. It is called the bell of the Dharma, the bell of the teaching.

We should take especial note that it is called the bell of the Dharma—the teaching—and not the bell of the Sangha—the work community—or the bell of the Buddha—the teacher, because it is a demonstration of the method of awakening and transformation, a vivid portrait of something to be accomplished through a definite method.

Rubbing the edge of the bell, a vibration begins and, once the bell is vibrating at full pitch and resonance, we must continue rubbing the edge of the bowl without interrupting the vibration if we wish the vibration to persist.

If we are careless, inattentive or hesitant, we will break the flow and the ringing will cease. We must then begin afresh. We must continue this exercise until we are able to make the bell ring and keep it ringing indefinitely.

If we lose the vibration, the singing bowl must be brought slowly and carefully back up past a definite barrier, a threshold of vibration before it will again produce the full sound. It is not easy to make the bowl really sing and, like a woman's awakening, requires patience and subtlety.

Another demonstration used by schools to visualize the process of bringing the machine to life is the Japanese

Shakuhachi. The Shakuhachi is a type of flute. It can be made of bamboo, rosewood, maple, mahogany or even plastic.

The easiest of all to play is the plastic flute, and its sound is perfectly adequate for ordinary music. However, the real Shakuhachi is a teaching mechanism and is difficult to play.

The bamboo Shakuhachi with a root base is the true teaching instrument, because only perfect effortless breathing and no-mind mindfulness—which we call pure presence and the unremitting attention powered by the essential higher emotion of adoration—will produce a vibrant and mellow sound from it.

The Shakuhachi teaches how to breathe a perfect breath, how to breathe one's last breath into the flute, as if giving one's final breath to death, the ultimate lover.

All of these devices are vivid examples of the quality and heightened level of vibration of an awakened machine.

They all illustrate that the awakened machine requires constant attention and presence, with an inexorable but gentle pressure, powered by the subtle force of adoration.

We learn from the singing bowl and the Shakuhachi that the machine will go dead—fall back into sleep—the very moment that attention, which has brought it to life, falters or is withdrawn, even momentarily.

If we consciously adore the machine, it will respond by reflex to our adoration with a profound higher emotion. This higher emotion with which the machine answers our adoration brings about our own transformation.

E.J. Gold, Penetration Is The Aim, Charcoal on Rives BFK, 1996

E.J. Gold, They Can Take Nothing From Me , Charcoal Arches 1990

CHAPTER 16

Attack at Dawn: A Beachhead into the Fourth Dimension

In our beginning work, we often attempt to accomplish too much at once. Our efforts are scattered and our energy quickly dissipates itself. We must discipline ourselves to improve the quality and potency of our efforts by condensing them at first.

In our beginning work, because we are excited about the prospects, we are probably trying to do too much at once. Our efforts, because of their frequency, diminish in force and are not effective.

Our attention wanders here and there, or is distracted by many inner and outer influences, and we do not seem to have much will to awaken the machine in spite of our serious work efforts.

Our attention becomes scattered when we work with too many exercises and we insist on dissipating our energies toward work efforts during the entire day.

We can condense our efforts during the day into one major effort at one definite time each day, until we get a good grip on it.

If we could only take one thing with us to a desert island it should be the method for awakening the human biological machine. We would need nothing else to realize the full potential of life in a human biological machine. With this method, which does not require special external conditions, we could accomplish everything possible for a human being.

If we were locked away in a room with only a single chair, plain white walls and a bare light bulb, even if we were a fish in a tank, we could still do our work if we knew how to awaken the machine without the need for special exercises.

Even if the machine were helpless in bed, we would still have the machine's perceptions, memories and sensations, and as long as we have the machine itself, we have everything we need for our possible evolution.

If we understood the machine's perceptions, states and sensations, we would know whether it is awake or asleep, and could, if we knew how, act upon this information just by placing our will of attention upon the machine, regardless of its state or condition, to awaken the machine and utilize its transformational function.

But the main point is that, if we intend to try to awaken the machine we must not do anything else at the same time. We must place a pure hermetic seal upon the time we have set aside for this effort. We have got to make up our minds that we will tolerate no distraction during this time.

This firm decision, which tolerates no exception whatever, is the only discipline we need at this time.

Even with an untrained attention, anyone ought to be able to set aside five minutes a day during which nothing else enters to distract or attract the attention—no outside worries, no business concerns, no anticipation of the day's problems, no nervous agitation, no upsets, no daily problems, no emotional outbursts, no arguments, no amusements, no entertainment— just for five minutes out of a whole day!

When we first begin, we establish an exact, very short, period of time that we know we can set aside without distractions. Boiling the work-time down to a mere five minutes serves to help us extract the essence of a whole day's effort.

A very short but definite period of work is like establishing a beachhead, a foothold, on strange territory.

In a sense, we are establishing a beachhead in the Fourth Dimension, hoping to someday build a colony in this strange new world.

We must not bite off more than we can chew or the beachhead will be defeated. We must not try to do too much at once, if we expect to see results.

If we work along too many different lines at once, we become confused, our work loses force and our efforts lose potency.

We must set aside the same exact time-period every day, to the exact second—then we know that every day we have a certain amount of time to work—and only that short amount of time—during which time we are to try to awaken the machine, thinking of nothing else, doing nothing else, worrying about nothing else.

If the time period is not too long, our whole, undistracted and unwandering attention should be able to focus on this effort without fail.

Between these periods of effort from one day to the next, we must not allow ourselves to work to awaken the machine, even accidentally. We must allow the machine to run wild, to do anything it wishes, but the period for work is sacred, sacrosanct—inviolable. We must hold the beachhead totally secure against any distraction if we hope to gain any ground whatever.

This works best if we agree with ourselves to hold this beachhead at the same time *every day*, without fail. We must not lose our foothold on the Fourth Dimension by wandering away from our beachhead even for one day, or we are forced to begin again, not at the same point we began, but lower, because we have exposed a serious weakness.

Because we are concentrating our effort into just five minutes, we increase the potency of our effort. After all, we have a full twenty-three hours, fifty-five minutes and four seconds remaining to us each day to gather our energy for this single five-minute effort, if we do not waste our energy in fidgeting, nervous activity, worry, anxieties, insecurities, vanities, exhilarating sports, and other forms of negativity. It is the *potency* of effort that we are interested in.

Of course, during this annoying five-minute work obligation, we will miss many of our habits of life, but we must ask ourselves which life is more important—where our true priorities are—and whichever is highest, be it our work or our ordinary habits, we must do the one and give up the other from then on.

We must also find a way to pay for—to value—those precious five minutes of work each day. After all, we intend to allow ourselves only five minutes each day *and no longer* to work to awaken the machine.

We must find a way to value this time in much the same way that we value money, whether we are aware of it or not. We must find a way to pay for this time—especially if we do not use it for our work, even if we do not profit from it because we have wasted our energy on other concerns, or have dissipated ourselves in worry, agitation or negative emotion.

We will be so frustrated during the twenty-three hours, fifty-five minutes and four seconds we are not allowed to work to awaken the machine that the frustration should act as a dynamo, building the potency for our beachhead in the fourth dimension, generating the force for our attack at dawn.

This does not mean that we should not withhold outbursts of negativity. Our number-one rule in work is that we may not allow ourselves to manifest negatively. Withholding manifestations of negativity for the purpose of accumulating inner alchemical heat is an expected norm in a work community, and the stress-related ailments which inevitably result are just another hazard of work toward transformation.

Because we are attempting to increase the potency of our effort, we must respect each other's storage battery, each other's storage capacitor. We are accumulating energy for a five-minute work period for the following day. We are not to deplete each other's work force.

Ordinarily, we rob each other's work energy by drawing others into our negative states. Even if we do not take others' work energy directly, we force it out of them by forcing them to become participants in our negative states. This is a form of emotional rape.

We must respect each other's capacity to accumulate force, to gather the greatest possible potency; this is the only strategy we really need for work.

Theft or rape are crimes against a person's work. If we do this to ourselves, we are raping and robbing ourselves. The shock of realization of the grave consequences of our negative behavior can assist us in gaining the artificial will necessary to remember our intention to awaken the machine.

During this time, we will keep a work-diary, a record of combat against the will of the machine. This diary is obligatory, and no one is exempt. In the diary we will keep notes about what was and was not effective, what we think might have worked, and so on.

Once we have established the beachhead, we can expand our invasion into the Fourth Dimension. We can think of ourselves as an invasion force, receiving our pre-invasion briefing the evening before D-Day.

Each of us will land in the five-minute, take a five-minute piece of territory, and establish a firm beachhead. Once we have established the beachhead and stabilized the situation, we will begin to expand our operation; we will coordinate our invasion force and link up our beachheads, then expand our invasion further into the Fourth Dimension.

Of course there are always casualties; the majority of casualties in any invasion is always on the beach. During the remainder of the day, when we are not working to awaken the machine, we can study the machine, evaluate the sleep of the machine and see how difficult it would be to extend our beachhead into this enemy territory. Does the machine have frequent emotional storms? Is it very deeply asleep? How committed is it to its habits?

We may observe the machine on a total rampage, and for the first time we may realize that eventually, someday, sooner or later, we are expected to awaken the machine during the rampage, every single moment of it.

We can use our time to begin our evaluation of the sleep of the machine, the life of the machine, how much will it exerts over the situation, how difficult the terrain.

We probably already have a good idea of which territories, which states, are going to be difficult.

As a general rule of thumb, the more the will of the machine is exerted over the situation, the more resistant it will be toward its awakening.

What is worse, if it happened once, it is likely that we will encounter that same terrain many, many times in the life of the machine.

Spend the day evaluating the sleep of the machine and evaluating how difficult it would be, by asking yourself specifically, "Well, how hard would it be to wake the machine up in this situation? What kind of problems is the machine making for me here?"

In a sense, we are gathering military intelligence to expand our beachhead with the purpose of eventually extending our invasion. Where before we were gathering evidence that an invasion was necessary, now we are gathering intelligence, information which we can use to extend our invasion into the Fourth Dimension.

Remember that our aim right now is to establish a beachhead and at the same time to study the machine's activities—to gather the necessary intelligence to expand and extend the beachhead.

This is no joke. For five minutes every day we will literally hold territory in another dimension, a dimension about which we know absolutely nothing.

The only weapon the essential self has is the will of attention. A small weapon, a subtle weapon, but a very powerful weapon over a period of time. It is gentle but as inexorable as the waves of the ocean upon a rock.

Eventually, all rock is reduced to dust. Just by the gentle but unremitting action of water. The gentle action of unremitting attention has the same ability to grind down even the rock of Gibraltar into dust, sooner or later...mostly later, but this is the way with all noncathartic methods.

Eventually, time grinds every grain. Just the inexorable power of unremitting attention will awaken the machine from its slow death. The awakening will spread like fire under the unremitting gentle but inexorable attention, just as the greatest of geological formations eventually gives way to the inexorable action of wind and water.

If we understand this simple principle, then we understand the very basis of zen. The only weapon we really have or need is the gentle erosion of the sleep of the machine under the inexorable pressure of the wind and water of attention.

E.J. Gold, Sharp Observation, Charcoal on Rives BFK, 1987

E.J. Gold, Did You Call My Name? , Charcoal on Arches 1990

CHAPTER 17

Warming of the Soul

Growth of the soul requires a form of human sacrifice, the exact nature of which has long since been distorted in mainstream thought. Evolutionary barriers—flaws in the diamond—are ground down by abrasion.

We can think of the essential self as a diamond which can be cut and polished until it develops certain definite tendencies which enable it to enter the Work.

We may think of a diamond as too hard to cut, but it can be, or we would not see multifaceted stones such as the brilliant and perfection cuts common to contemporary engagement sets.

Although a diamond can be broken with a chisel to make a rough cut, it can only be ground into exact faceting by another diamond, actually many small diamonds acting as a kind of sandpaper.

Of course, if the stone had a flaw, and it were up to the

flaw, the flaw would be in the center of the stone. But a diamond cutter cannot think like this; the flaw must be sacrificed.

We may lose some weight in the diamond, but it will be more valuable as a smaller but better diamond.

But first, before we can even cut the diamond, we must remove the raw stone from its matrix, composed of dirt and much softer rock.

To remove the matrix, we use what we call friction—a preparatory technique—to reveal the stone in the rough, applying a variety of techniques.

People in the mainstream of human life commonly confuse schools with psychological communities, because essentially the same techniques are used to remove the matrix and reveal the rough stone within.

But then—and this is where ordinary psychology and philosophy fails—they feel that once the rough stone is revealed and the diamond is free from the matrix, it is perfect; or, to obtain additional fees from their clients, they may continue to stubbornly continue cutting the matrix long after the rough diamond is revealed.

Only if the diamond is free from the matrix can the abrasive process take place. Once the stone is revealed, we are no longer interested in the matrix, so we discontinue our grinding process with the matrix.

For the matrix we use much softer tools, but if we expect to cut a diamond, we must use something equally hard; for this purpose we will use other diamonds as a polishing medium.

If we are like diamonds in our essence and the diamond can

be recut, then the great diamond of the Absolute, in whose image we know our essential selves to be made, can also be recut.

If we can think of the Absolute as a diamond, we can also think of the work community as a diamond. But what if we noticed a flaw in the community? If we obstruct others in our work community, we—the flaw in the community—must be cut away from the larger stone for the sake of the stone, even though it reduces the size of the stone, because a stone without flaws is increased in value.

Of course, small flaws need not be cut from the community. The flaw would have to be very serious.

Only seven possible serious flaws could appear in our community-diamond. Of these flaws we probably know anger the best; another serious flaw is hatred, and another flaw is uncontrolled lust. Most of us are already familiar with the seven deadly flaws.

If we cut those flaws out of our own diamond by abrasion with other diamonds, we are not so seriously flawed that we must be cut out of a community.

But if any of those flaws exist in us—resentment, hatred, anger, revulsion, disgust—to the extent that we actually interfere with the work of others—if conditions are still able to evoke in us wild and dangerous reflexes of negative emotion, then we are subject to removal from the larger stone, and it is neither our choice, nor the choice of a teacher.

We use the word *matrix* both in its lapidary sense, which is to say, that stone which encases a harder stone, and also in the sense of mother.

If we realize that a community is composed of those who have little or no matrix remaining around the stone—just raw, rough diamonds—we can easily understand the difference between ourselves and those in the larger community, who still have a great deal of matrix and are concerned with the things of the matrix, with changing the matrix, polishing the matrix and enhancing the matrix. Our stone has been exposed, and we are in the raw, ready for cutting and polishing.

The Great Work, the cutting of the Great Diamond, with our own diamond-like essential selves, is called the process of Redemption. It will require more than just we ourselves to accomplish this work and to become a part of this work, we must surrender ourselves to the work community.

If we hope to seriously take part in this work, we must, once and for all, give up the things of the matrix and reconcile ourselves to the seemingly endless grinding process, the cutting of the diamond.

In a work community, our diamond may be severely criticized; if we became upset at this we would realize at once that the stone has not yet been freed from the matrix, because only the matrix could become upset by criticism. In the diamond industry, another word for criticism is appraisal.

All serious flaws must be removed, and the more objective and ruthless the appraisal, the better. The best cutter will appraise the diamond absolutely ruthlessly, without consideration for the feelings of the flaws in the stone, seeing objectively and impartially what would be best to bring the stone to its fullest possible potential.

Let us try to experience what it will be like to polish the diamond once the psychological and emotional matrix has been removed...

We will imagine ourselves sitting cross-legged, holding a heavy ball of cold clay gently and lovingly in our cupped hands.

As our attention comes to rest upon the clay, we will imagine ourselves to have somehow suddenly ascended from one of the lower dimensions into a higher state in which the whole universe is visible, and to have taken the form of this clay which we now cradle in our hands.

Somehow, we do not know quite how, although only moments ago we were convinced that we were on the planet Earth, we now find ourselves viewing the universe from the outside.

In our present exalted state, we vaguely remember that if this "clay" is the universe, then its interior must be filled with trillions upon trillions of luminous bodies, stars and planets suspended in space, speeding outward away from one another by the force of mutually repellent gravitational fields, and that somewhere within this little universe is the almost unthinkably minuscule star around which our most recent place of habitation, the planet Earth, revolves.

We know that even with the aid of very big telescopes, those remaining inside the universe cannot see us outside the boundary of the clay, because, within the boundaries of the universe, the light bends and reflects, curving back upon itself.

The inside is entirely dark except for the pinpoint brightness of little stars swirling in their galactic clusters. Although it looks small to us now, we know that the distance across this little clay cosmos we hold in our hands is many light years.

We ourselves are connected in some way to this little universe; our consciousness flows through both forms, the Creator and the Creation, like a smoky vapour.

Now we are going to imagine that we very intensely regard this little clay cosmos in our hands. If we were still in the lower dimension, we would call this substance "clay", because it comes from the earth.

At first, until we understand more about it, we are going to penetrate inside it with our special vision and locate, somewhere among all the galactic clusters of stars, that little yellow star near which we will see the tiny spinning mudball from which we just came.

We will allow our vision to penetrate deep within the clay cosmos, far beyond where our ordinary vision can see, far down into the lower dimensions.

We are in no hurry; there is no passage of time here, so we can work with no feeling of urgency.

In order to concentrate the full force of our attention toward the penetration into the lower dimensions, we must recollect our full attention. If we have lost some part of our attention to our past, we will not have enough force of attention in the present. If we hope to accomplish our aim, we cannot afford to allow even a part of our attention to dwell in memories.

We will now collect all our past attention into the present. Some part of our attention also inevitably remains on the little world in the lower dimensions for which we are searching with our penetrating vision.

We will leave some of our attention there to help guide our

154

vision.

But we might also find some of our attention on our job or on our bills that we need to pay, or on our money. We cannot afford to lose our precious attention to such trivia; and after all, what business do we have with salaries and rent, now that we find ourselves outside the Creation?

Because we require this attention for our penetrating vision, we have the right to bring it to the present for this purpose.

We may have friends, children, husbands, wives, fathers, mothers, sisters, brothers, cousins, and others whom we have left behind us who felt??? that they need??? us, but just now, in this circumstance, we are of no help to them and, in any case, we cannot afford to spare this attention.

Because of our necessity, we are entitled to bring this attention to our present aim.

Undoubtedly we also have some attention on the future, even if it is nothing more than general worry about what will become of us and our life. But we are far from that life now, and we will need every bit of attention we can muster.

We will bring this attention also to the present.

We might have some attention on our personal hungers, cravings, fears, discomforts, and even upon exactly how we feel about our present situation.

Our hungers and also our insecurities about ourselves— our vanities—even this little bit of attention cannot be spared from the task at hand. With a mentally visualized hand, we will lift our attention away from our personal vanities, and using this same visualized hand, we will replace the collected attention firmly upon this clay object as if attention were a tangible substance.

If we have missed or overlooked some attention, we can collect it now, just like a tangible substance, and place it into this object, as if the attention were an additional piece of living, palpitating clay.

We also no doubt have some part of our attention on our phenomenal accumulations back on that tiny little planet, whatever its name was...automobiles, clothing, knick-knacks, furniture, carpets, drapes, paintings, photographs, books, records, stereo equipment, television...

Naturally, we have superstitiously held some part of our attention on them to guard them mentally against theft. If we take our attention from them, it is possible they may be stolen, but that is the risk we must take.

We may return to an empty apartment, but we cannot afford to waste this very big part of our attention, and we need it *now*.

We will lift the attention from the objects we have accumulated, and push it into this clay substance we hold in what we call our hands.

To this universe we are like a God. But if we hope to do anything with this Creation, even God needs all the attention possible.

If some part of our attention still remains on something— anything other than the immediate necessity—we must collect it at once, in the same way that we would pick up pieces of clay which have dropped on the floor.

We will hold this clay cosmos in the steady gaze of our unremitting attention and eventually, as the mood strikes us, we will imagine ourselves forming it slowly into some interesting shape, using the laws of artistic accident.

We suddenly recognize that this object, because it is the object of the totality of our collected and concentrated attention, is now actually the sum total of our whole attention, of which we are the source...that we are now looking at a living embodiment of our own attention.

This clay substance, when infused with the whole of our attention, is called the *soul*, which we hope to help to grow, evolve, and infuse with life.

Just now it seems to be inanimate, lifeless, just clay. This moment would be a good opportunity, since we happen to hold it in our hands before us, and can see it quite easily, to feed it, to nurture it, to give it nourishment.

Let us imagine ourselves doing just this. We will think of nothing else but providing it with nourishment, with our life-force.

We will discover that obstacles to this effort will arise in ourselves, but we can move them aside by mental *Tai Chi* or emotional *Jujitsu*. Considerations must not interfere.

It happens only rarely that we have an opportunity to perform this work of soul-warming. We may never have another chance in our whole life. So we must use the opportunity now to help our soul to grow, first by warming it.

The soul is cold. It has not had nourishment for a long time. We imagine ourselves studying it as we would study a lover, which is to say, our attention is completely rooted. We cannot seem to draw our attention away from our soul, even for an instant.

We will use every breath to give it life. Our attention must not stray, must not wander.

Our feelings toward this soul are very important. It will warm according to our love...our adoration... devotion...our radiance to it.

We warm the soul by setting ourselves on fire, a deep, slow alchemical fire, feeding the soul with our own precious life force.

We are consumed in this process, but we do not consider ourselves for a moment. The growth of the soul requires human sacrifice. We must allow it to consume us. We are the albumen; we will give our lives that our beloved might live.

We do not do this entirely for altruistic reasons. If we have studied, then we know the benefit to ourselves. Without this process, we know that we will be dead long before we die.

We may pass through many different moods as we warm the soul. We may just hold it, or draw it to the breast and stroke it; we may warm each part by wandering touch, dance with it, study its visible form, hear it, feel it.

The warming force is called love—not romantic love, not sentimental love, but the force which *is* love, which is to say, that-which-warms.

As the soul is warmed, we lose our own life-force in the form of heat. As the beloved becomes warmer than us, then we become like clay, we lose our life and die. In effect, our genuine nature has been absorbed by the soul.

This is the secret of transformation: that our life-force learns to leave the rough clay of the body and enter and give life to the finer clay of the soul.

Before this, there is no soul; as we see, the soul is just a lump of cold clay.

Through our sacrifice, the soul will live and at the same time, as we die, we pass to the soul, where we are resurrected.

We will bring the soul close to the solar plexus and when it begins to throb, when it feels hot, we will allow it to absorb our force as though feeding itself through an umbilical cord.

We must feed it with the life-force from many, many such bodies as these, for a very, very long time, until it is fully developed.

We can accelerate its growth and evolution by giving freely of ourselves and by awakening the machine. If we have not lost our energy through negative states and manifestations, we can accumulate much more of this life force than would be produced in the ordinary course of nature.

Slowly, slowly, we will withdraw, replacing the soul in the lap gently, very slowly. It is sleeping now. We will imagine that we have put the soul away until next time.

We do not know if we will be able to do this again soon or only after a very long time. It might be tomorrow, or it might be one hundred thousand years, but at least we have done a little today.

E.J. Gold, Something Marvelous , Charcoal on Arches 1990

CHAPTER 18

Out of Body

Once we are able to bring the machine to stillness and silence, we will experience ourselves as definitely separate from the machine with a life apart from and far beyond the life of the machine.

Here is an experiment that has been devised to help us dissociate ourselves from our bodies and from the sensations of our bodies:

We are going to discover in this experiment a whole body of knowledge unavailable to the majority of human beings, because they are entrapped by their taboos. They are not allowed forbidden knowledge.

Life has a way of keeping this knowledge from someone who is not seriously pursuing it, yet someone who is seriously pursuing it cannot be stopped from obtaining it. If we really want it, we need only cross over the line.

161

Diffused vision is the key to the out-of-body experience. At some point, we will open our eyes, diffuse our vision, and find that looking down we have no legs, no body, no arms. This will most certainly happen to us if we pursue this seriously. Strange things are going to start happening.

As we begin to provoke certain states and certain visions, real phenomena will begin to occur, also hallucinatory false phenomena will be generated. Do not discount everything just because there is a lot of false phenomena. Some things are genuine.

When this material is running well and the false phenomena have dropped away leaving what is genuine, we are ready to work in the more dangerous domains.

Right now, what we are doing is safe, but at some point we will have to leave the safety of the island and launch out to more dangerous realms. Not now, and not until we are very skilled.

We want the machine to become completely relaxed. During this experiment, we must not allow movement to continue in the machine, except for the necessary life-support systems of heartbeat and respiration.

We do not wish to allow movement or anything else which will bring our awareness back to the machine's sensations. We want to lose the sensation of being in the machine.

Once we have been able to bring the machine to stillness and silence, we will be able to use a very ancient trick to experience ourselves as something which is very definitely separate from the machine and which has its life apart from and far beyond the life of the machine.

162

Seating ourselves before a full-length mirror, with all electrical lights and appliances turned off and a dark candle—because we want no distractions from the sight of the candle itself—burning off to one side, behind the back or in front on the floor—whichever works best—we should follow this as if it were expressing thoughts in our own mind:

"I want to get the idea that what I see before me is not a reflection, but the machine itself, that I am a nothingness, a mere reflection of the machine, viewing the machine suspended in midair or through a doorway between dimensions.

"I must convince myself that I am not in the machine, that I am viewing the machine from outside.

"I remember having been in the machine, but now I am looking at it from outside, and it looks very strange to me—very peculiar. It is not at all what I thought it was when I was in it.

"I must not allow my penetrating gaze to wander from the sight of the machine for a single instant; I immerse myself in the feeling of mild surprise that I was able to leave the machine so easily, and that because I am finally free from the machine's own view of itself, I see my life in the machine very differently than I did when I was inside it.

"I very quickly realize that none of this is imaginary, that I really am outside the machine, looking at what I always considered to be myself.

"Isn't it odd what a different view of myself I have, now that I am outside the machine?

"When I was inside it, I thought of myself as looking quite

different. But, now that I am outside, I see the machine totally objectively, as others would see the machine.

"Isn't it strange to be looking into my own eyes, studying my own face? The brain is still in there, working away, just thinking about its own thoughts, and thinking about its own feelings. Isn't it refreshing to have left that behind?

"I have parked the body, gotten outside of it. This is a unique opportunity to study it objectively from outside. What size does it seem to be? What is it feeling?

"I wonder what sensations are coursing through it right now...what feelings are reverberating through it? As I study the machine, I feel some compassion for it, because it is mortal, it will someday die.

"I know that it has pain, it has its own thoughts, it has its own hopes and fears; it has sadness, happiness, and sickness.

"I know that it has these things because I have shared them with the machine for a very long time now.

"The machine taught me all about these things. It has taught me pleasure and pain; from the machine I have learned to pursue the future, to hope for things to come, to long for the past, to put my faith in activities, ideas, and feelings.

"The machine looks rather strange and empty without me inside it. It seems to have a life of its own. Its breathing and heartbeat go on as usual. It could easily go about its business without me, and no one would ever be the wiser, no one would ever need to know that I was not inside the machine, if I decided not to return to it.

"What difference would it make if I did or didn't go back in there, since I have nothing to do with the thoughts, feelings, or sensations of the body anyway?

"And not only does the machine provide all its own thoughts, feelings and sensations, it also makes its own decisions. How wonderful for me—a machine that just does everything itself!

"Really I am very lucky, because I need not concern myself with the business of the machine. My interference is unnecessary. It is an automatic machine.

"I wonder what it is thinking now...Let me take stock of what I see, starting with the apparent size of the object. What size is it, actually? When viewed from outside, not in relation to any of its artifacts, it doesn't seem to have any particular size.

"It seems neither alive nor deads,　just a machine, something carved out of soft stone, an energy sculpture...a solid mathematical equation...

"Just an empty container which does not seem capable of anything,　it seems absurd to think of it as anything that can have thoughts and feelings.

"I suddenly realize how these thought-patterns I am having now are a result of having been immersed in the sleep of the machine, how much I have been conditioned to think and feel like the machine.

"Looking at the machine from out here, I can see that it does not have much time to work; it never did have much time from the beginning. What a feeling of relief not to be stuck in there any more, not to be confined...

"The machine has been programmed and conditioned by life to remain asleep, not to function as a transformational apparatus. If I return to it, I will have to help it to overcome all sorts of social taboos and psychological fears which it has accepted and which were intended to keep the machine in sleep.

"The machine looks as if it has suffered a great deal, and has spent a lot of time doing things that it didn't like, and that were uncomfortable.

"I have the feeling that this is something like what I will experience when the machine dies; I'll turn around and look at the dead machine, and this is more or less what it will look like.

"I know that if I cannot get the machine to function as a transformational apparatus, I will be drawn into it again...

"I know that if everything continues the way it is going now, my tendency will be to return to it, and at the moment of its death, I will probably want to return to its moment of birth, staying in it again all the way through its life from birth to death...

"From this vantage point, the machine appears extremely simple, yet ridiculously sophisticated and complicated, and then the vision changes.

"From here, I can see some unexpected things that I never thought I would look at or consider.

"If I can stay out of the machine a little longer, the reverberations, thoughts, feelings and sensations of the machine will surely die away.

"I find myself looking at it as if I were viewing some alien thing, but, I suppose because I have just gotten out of it and started looking at it, I continue to think like the machine, feel

166

like the machine, have sensations like the machine, beliefs like the machine, and attitudes like the machine.

"At times I feel as if I will want to return to its life, or that even if I want to remain outside it or go elsewhere, I might be drawn back into it by sheer force of habit and mutual electrical attraction.

"When I first saw the machine from out here, I felt an incredible love and compassion toward it, but now that I have been out of it for a while, I feel absolutely emotionless about this empty shell, this thing, sitting there in front of me...no compassion or love toward it, at least in the ordinary way.

"I feel love but not as the machine knows it...impartial love, love without sensation, love without an object.

"As I take stock of the situation, I notice that there is a subtle difference in my focus, my outlook...because I am temporarily free from the life of the machine, I am aware of a different dimension outside my usual perception, even though what I see is more or less the same.

"I must try to remember that the key to all this is in the diffusion of my vision, which gives me the means to achieve the annihilation of the illusion of perspective which produces the hallucinatory vision of dimensionality, of volume, depth, and distance.

"I want to achieve the nondimensional vision which comes when I allow the vision to relax, not trying to look at anything specific. I want to open my vision as wide as possible but not focused on anything in particular.

"Now I am starting a phase, in which I begin projecting an intense feeling of adoration for the machine which I see before me as I float free in space.

"It is hard to remember that it is just a machine, that it is entirely mechanical, that it has no life of its own, unless I give it life, bring it to life with waves of adoration.

"This is natural to me, to send waves of adoration toward the machine, and as the machine comes to life, it will return the adoration, which I will gratefully bring in to myself, add to it and send some more. Bring it back, add to it and send it again, wave after wave of adoration.

"I am both the giver and the receiver. The giving is the getting. What goes around comes around. The machine can only return adoration as it receives adoration, and as I receive it, I add to it.

"Adoration of the machine gives it life, like touching something electrical which flows into the heart, a low voltage shock. More attention is needed, to give it more adoration. I pour adoration into the machine in ever-increasing waves, building slowly to an almost unbearable crescendo..."

E.J. Gold, Sleeping or Awake?, Charcoal on Rives BFK, 1987

E.J. Gold, Clinging to the Content of the Mind, Charcoal Arches 1987

CHAPTER 19

The Chronic Defense Mechanism

Because of its fear of not being able to reintegrate the sleeping state, the machine has learnt to defend itself against the waking state. Each individual has a particular defense mechanism called the Chronic which is triggered off whenever the machine is threatened with awakening.

The machine's Chronic is another name for the machine's defense mechanism, which acts as a warning that the machine is near or about to enter the waking state and, at the same time, defends the machine against the waking state.

Suppose we see that anger is our typical state. We could deduce from this that anger may be our machine's defense mechanism against the waking state.

We would soon see that this defense mechanism which we call the Chronic activates itself automatically, but only when the machine's established routine—which maintains its precarious balance—is threatened by the waking state.

The nearer the waking state, the more profound the manifestations produced by the defense mechanism. Then, when the waking state no longer threatens, the defense mechanism tends to subside.

As the waking state is approached more closely, the Chronic will manifest itself more and more dramatically.

The barrier between the sleeping state and the waking state is maintained by the Chronic. We actually are quite frequently near the waking state, often bumping into the waking state without actually crossing over the line.

In fact, as children, most of us were in the waking state most of the time; that is, before the Chronic was developed by the machine to defend itself against the waking state so that it would be able to function acceptably in a social and cultural context.

Social, economic and cultural functionings are governed by the sleeping state. If things were otherwise, the elements of social existence would not be important.

The machine develops the Chronic in the first place because if the machine were to fall into the waking state and remain in the waking state, the events of daily life would take on little or no meaning.

We would find ourselves in the midst of a vast, bizarre and extremely hilarious comedy. The cultural imperatives would seem extremely funny, and we would view the social necessities as meaningless and ironically zany.

The test of this idea can be proven by the fact that those who are able to enter the waking state often do so with peals of helpless mirth.

If we examine the laughter and the purpose of the laughter as rejection of paradox, we will see that it generally indicates that we have taken a look at the sleeping state and find the pursuits of the sleeping state unimportant and even totally nonexistent in relation to the raw reality of the waking state.

In recognition of this, the machine has developed an automatic defense mechanism against the waking state, which often takes the form of some Chronic negative emotion such as anger, sarcasm, cynicism, self-isolation, fear, paranoia, hysteria, resentment, envy, pettiness, jealousy, vengefulness, greed, piety, boredom, grief, loneliness, anxiety, helplessness, stupidity, hatred, compulsiveness, and so on, so that it can continue to function with significance and importance according to the expectations of others.

When we view the machine as something which is actually functioning correctly in the sleeping state, as far as its survival in the ordinary sense is concerned, we will have compassion, recognizing the wisdom of the machine in its development of the Chronic as a defense mechanism against the waking state so that it can maintain the sleeping state and therefore function properly from the cultural view.

If we want to discover our Chronic, all we have to do is go into horizontal sleep and have somebody shake us awake in the wee hours of the night or sometime in the pre-dawn and observe our first reaction. *That* will be our Chronic.

The machine doesn't want to enter the waking state. It knows instinctively that it will have a difficult time reassembling the sleeping state and resuming its social functions. At the same time, it's just like a child who at first won't go into the bathtub, then after playing in the tub a while, doesn't want to get out.

The machine doesn't want to enter the waking state; it resists it right up to the last moment. But once it's in the waking state, it can't *imagine* what it was ever doing in the sleeping state, why it preferred the sleeping state, why it developed a defense mechanism against this wonderful waking state, and may even wish never to return to the sleeping state again.

But when it has returned once again to the sleeping state, it can't imagine what it ever saw in the waking state, and it wants to stay where it is now just as powerfully as it wanted to remain in the waking state a few moments or hours ago.

The machine naturally tends toward homeostasis—the impulse to remain where it is and to stabilize the existing condition.

The machine's ultimate goal is to achieve the steady state and remain there without change from then on, forever, if possible. An undisturbed and unchanging routine in which nothing new is ever introduced, is the machine's idea of Heaven.

From our previous studies of the machine in the waking state, we realize that in the waking state the machine no longer has will, in the sense that it no longer has the force to enforce its own patterns of behavior and direction, because the machine's will depends upon the motor centrum which functions with the force of negative emotion, and negative emotion cannot exist in the waking state.

In the waking state, the machine is in the same condition it would be in if it were hypnotized, which is to say, devoid of machine imperatives and the force necessary to impose them.

174

Ordinarily, the machine in its early experiences in the waking state tends to just sit or stand quietly and do nothing, or pace nervously up and down or back and forth, or slump over in the "pity-me-slouch", depending on its tendencies.

In most people, the defense mechanism developed very strongly at about five years, before which it did not appear.

Once the defense mechanism is firmly established, we can become automatically functioning members of our sophisticated tribal culture, true adults in the most poignant sense of the word.

The defense mechanism was allowed to develop in the machine, but why? Only because somebody we implicitly trusted encouraged us to develop the defense mechanism against the waking state and to grow up—in a particular way —to adopt certain habits and make behavior modifications and so forth.

Trusted individuals in our life—parents, teachers, peers, uncles and aunts and others who were close to us—gave us, in fact, almost all those conditioning impulses—control-commands—which form the defense mechanism.

It is this conditioning and the necessity for a completely automatic operation of the machine which produced the need for the sleeping state.

The defense mechanism was developed by the machine to keep the sleeping state in place, and eventually the sleeping state took the form of the defense mechanism, which further automatized the effect.

The defense mechanism manifests in behavior, in posture, in expression, and even in goals and purposes.

Because we trusted these people, we did not resist the inhibitions and imposition of unnatural and even obviously mechanical goals, ideals and attitudes which they imposed upon us in much the same way that a child would typically be victimized by a child molester who is a close member of the family, but in this case even though the molestation is on a psychoemotional, and not a physical level, the damage is no less severe.

This conditioning might have been imposed in a variety of ways; for instance, we might see uncle Arnold in a vivid demonstration of reflexive anger which seems to have an effect. This anger reflex might eventually become the deep core around which the defense mechanism would be formed.

The defense mechanism serves a variety of functions in our relations with others and with ourselves, and without it we would find ourselves completely nonfunctional in our ordinary life.

As we discovered ourselves to be nonfunctional in the waking state, we would have naturally allowed the machine to assume those social and cultural functionings which we found impossible or meaningless in the waking state.

This takeover of the machine would typically be completed by the age of about five years, and a second level of conditioning would occur once more at about eleven years.

But what happens to the defense mechanism once the machine is in the waking state? The machine only defends itself against the waking state while it is in the sleeping state. No point closing the barn door after the horse is stolen.

Again, remember why the machine defends itself against the waking state in the first place. After the brief respite of the waking state, it will be forced to restructure the functional sleeping state. When we can assure ourselves that we can re-enter the sleeping state whenever we wish, we will be far less reluctant to leave the sleeping state and enter the waking state. If we have the key for reintegration of the sleeping state, we also have the key to achieving the waking state.

In a sense, the intentional disintegration and reintegration of the sleeping state is the key to the waking state. When we are able to freely leave the sleeping state, enter the waking state and then leave the waking state and re-enter the sleeping state, the machine will no longer fear the waking state, and the defense mechanism will slowly disarm itself, almost effortlessly.

This idea and its resulting methods have found expression in many teachings, from the shamanism of the Aurignacian Period to Tibetan Buddhism and Western monasticism.

The machine must be able to view the waking state without fear—the fear that it might be trapped in the waking state forever.

We can use the sleeping state to learn to solve the problems of the waking state, and to prepare ourselves to accomplish the Work, which is what we call that which is of real value from the viewpoint of the waking state, hoping to someday enter the permanent waking state.

The sleeping state has its definite value. After all, had we remained forever in the waking state, we could never have had the necessity for a school, because we would not be suffering in the sleeping state—which, after all, is our real motivation for seeking a school in the first place.

The point is that without special work on ourselves in the

sleeping state, we cannot remain in the waking state for very long. Eventually we descend into the sleeping state, and unless we have found a school in the lower dimensions, we have no way of knowing that the method by which we can learn to tolerate and function in the waking state is hidden in the sleeping state in the same way that a pearl is hidden in an oyster.

Ironically, the key to awakening is actually hidden in the sleeping state.

The determined—and successful—pursuit of the waking state eventually and inevitably activates the Chronic, making someone who is working on himself about as pleasant to live with as an angry camel.

Naturally the machine avoids the waking state because it *dreads* having to put the meaning of its ordinary existence back together again. The sleeping state has to be reconstructed each time from the waking state. It is all shattered and fragmented into what the Buddhists call *skandas*, which is to say, its primary components.

This is what the mysterious *Bardo Thodol* is all about: the maintenance of the waking state by the intentional and knowing reintegration of the primary components of the sleeping state.

Using special techniques, these can be made to periodically shatter just so they can be intentionally reconstructed—in the process of rebirth. We can learn to take ourselves apart and put ourselves together again, like Dodgson's Rosicrucian myth of Humpty Dumpty.

The machine wishes to avoid the fragmentation, the loss of face of the waking state, because to the machine, the waking state is like death.

Ritual and some forms of theatre, particularly mime, can actually help us to produce good habits of intentional reintegration of the sleeping state.

Only then, when we know how to consciously produce the sleeping state, will the machine no longer fear the waking state.

The essential self, of course, does not fear the waking state; it prefers it, while the machine will do anything it can to avoid it, fighting tooth and nail, clutching and grasping at every lamppost and doorjam that happens to present itself on the way to the waking state, like James Cagney as the big-shot no longer wisecracking gangster who falls into total hysteria as he's being dragged down the corridor of Death Row toward the green door.

Then once in the waking state, it will relax, and all the piss-and-vinegar will go out of the machine.

Although the Chronic also serves the sleeping state, the whole of the sleeping state with all its activities, attitudes and aims, also serves to reinforce the Chronic.

The maintenance of the sleeping state is the most important goal or purpose of the machine until it comes to a school, if, indeed, it ever does.

If we ask anyone on the street, "What is the purpose of your existence?", they will give an answer which translates roughly to, "My whole purpose in existing is to maintain the sleeping state of the machine."

Another name for the Chronic defense mechanism is *Chief Weakness*, but never mind what name we give it; it all boils down to *how the machine defends itself against the waking state*.

In the waking state, all the elements of sleep, all those things which make us suffer under their dominant force, will be absent.

The Chronic and everything that serves the Chronic will be absent. This should give us the clue that *the Chronic—and everything which serves the Chronic—actually forms the sleeping state*.

Unlike hypnotism, in the natural waking state there is no external source of will and therefore, when the machine enters the waking state, it tends to come to a grinding halt, because there's no one out there to tell it what to do, and no hint from inside, either.

At this point, the machine is in danger of being conditioned by an external source of will. There have been political and religious systems which took advantage of the fact that external will can be imposed upon a machine which has been brought into a temporary waking state through shock and strong emotion, in the same way that a hypnotist can impose his or her will, except that in the case of the hypnotist, the waking state also was imposed from outside.

Even though this idea may not be understood in so many words by politicians, and the technical details were never actually discovered, the practical aspects *were* understood sufficiently to produce definite effects in Nazi Germany and in the prisoner-of-war camps of North Korea.

The point is that, if an ordinary hypnotist can bring the machine into a waking state and then impose external will upon it, there must also be a way of *forcefully* preventing the

Chronic defense mechanism from activating.

The waking state and the hypnotic state are related—the only serious difference is that in the waking state there is no hypnotist, but in both cases, the methods of bringing the machine into the waking state are more or less the same.

Almost every method of producing the waking state takes advantage of the fact that *it is possible to use artificial means to prevent the machine from using the Chronic to defend itself against the waking state.*

This effect can also be produced with psychoactive substances, but although the defense mechanism is effectively disarmed by drugs, the waking state is severely impaired.

But in any case, whether through hypnosis or self-produced efforts, we cannot successfully bring the machine into the waking state until the machine is absolutely convinced of its ability to reconstruct the sleeping state.

Part of a school's discipline is to learn several exact methods of reconstructing the sleeping state from the viewpoint of the waking state.

With the key to the sleeping state, we have eliminated the machine's primary objection to the waking state.

We can categorize people into definite typicalities according to their Chronic. In this school, we happen to separate them into eighteen distinct categories, but we could just as easily decide upon any number of categories which make sense to us and prove to be a workable shorthand system of viewing the various defense mechanisms.

E.J. Gold, Only One Thing to Remember , Charcoal on Arches 1987

CHAPTER 20

The Electrical Affinity of the Essential Self and the Machine

The relationship between the essential self and the machine is based on a seduction, an affinity—electrical in nature—between their electrical fields. Evolution thus means transformation of the electrical field of the essential self in such a way as to free it from this affinity.

Once the essential self's attention can be focused solidly on an electrically charged anomaly in the machine's electrical field, the attention of the essential self is sufficient to discharge the distortion and return that portion of the field to normal.

When the essential self becomes aware of—and properly identifies—the field distortion, the attention naturally descends upon it.

This is an important idea because the attention of the essential self is a low-grade cleansing radiation similar to that encountered in the waking state which has the effect of temporarily disarming the chronic, and at the same time, stimulating the waking state by reflex-response in the machine.

It is not necessary for us to know exactly what distortion is being corrected by this cleansing radiation of the force of attention.

We may or may not have a name for the distortion, see any significance in it, or visualize pictures associated with it, but when the full attention of the essential self is directed upon it, the field distortion will dissolve. Usually, however, we will envision some sort of mental and emotional pictures and moods associated with the distortion.

These mental associations are called *significance*; they are not the charge itself. The charge is not stored mentally. It is a direct functional impingement upon the electrical field.

Mental pictures are just a filing system, a way of assigning some graspable meaning to simple electrical potential so that the mental apparatus can keep track of the machine's field distortions in which memory is stored.

If the mental apparatus didn't assign meaning and significance to these electrical anomalies, it would have no way of recalling memory, because without significance, all field distortions look alike. After all, they're just lumps of energy in an energy field...a slight variation of gray in an ocean of gray.

Experience itself, especially experience within the space-time matrix, is a way of labeling something that is happening

184

to us on an electrical-mathematical level. Perceptual experience and analysis of our experience is just one of many possible ways of sorting it out, labeling it, and filing it.

Our whole voyage through time and space from birth to death and beyond is simply a way of labeling, storing, filing, and recovering what is happening to us. It is a way of seeing what is happening. We file our electrical experience in memory by assigning to each electrical event a definite, rememberable subjective tactile hallucination.

The electrical field of the machine has no meaning in itself...it's just a moving, swirling, ever-changing pool of dancing electrons, and things happen to the electrical field, forming electrical eddies, ridges and cataracts.

As this happens, tactile hallucinations explain what is happening electrically. Every event, no matter how real the tactile hallucination may seem in the subjective sense, is, in the physics sense, an electrical event completely devoid of any objective significance.

Every electrical event has duration. We can follow the event by following the hallucinations which are associated with it. We mustn't trust the hallucinations to tell us what really happened; we must trust the raw electrical memory itself, which we can follow if we have the training and disciplined skill to observe events in their pure electrical state.

An event is something which seems to occur on a physics level, but then when we examine it more closely, we see that it was actually on a mathematical level.

We can follow the exponential curve of the mathematical equation which represents the effect on the electrical field which we call the human biological machine, which has had a further effect by producing hallucinations, the significance of which form the subjective result which we call *personal experience*.

On the experiential level, we see and sense a variety of mental pictures, we seem to have significance for them, and we seem to have very real and very profoundly convincing sensations which are associated with the physical event. The event then is stored electrically, and the tactile hallucinations which we associate with it are also stored.

If we dwell on the hallucinations and the subjective significance of these hallucinations—what happened or what seems to have happened—the hallucination may diminish or seem to have less force, but the field distortion will tend to persist.

We are not really interested in the tactile hallucinations associated with field distortions. We use them simply as a way of keeping track of which field distortions we are dealing with at the moment.

Field distortions produce stress in the field, which in turn causes pain when we try to address the distortion again. We can release the stress with the cleansing radiation of attention, thus blowing away the electrical potential which is stored there and which makes the electrical impaction that causes the field distortion.

Field distortion is produced by the impingement of other electrical events which occurred in the past and which, because they seem similar, are brought into the event for comparison.

These other, seemingly similar events, are brought in by suggestion. Suggestibility takes on a very different meaning if we consider that suggestibility is what convinces us to bring something from the past into a present event to compare the present event with the past event because they seem similar.

For instance, this event may remind me of eight-hundred-and-ten seemingly similar events—all trying to occupy this same moment at the same time!

We all know that two or more things cannot occupy the same space at the same time, and that if they did, this would tend to crowd them beyond the tolerance limits of local space and time, which produces what physicists and engineers call *tweak*—another name for field-stress.

If we removed all the earlier seemingly similar events from the present event, there would be, in fact, no field-stress or distortion, because all the stress in the event is caused solely by the impingement of other events all trying to occupy the same space at the same time.

The event itself does not contain stress unless other events are brought into it. Even a very profound event, such as the electrical field of a baseball bat entering the electrical field of the machine with a great deal of impact and force would not, in and of itself, produce stress on the event, but because impingement is brought into the event, there is an overload, producing a reflex state of sleep which is commonly called unconsciousness.

In our beginning work, we are learning to bring the machine into the waking state, and at the same time, to remove sleep and the effects of the sleeping state from the entire lifetime.

We will do this in a variety of ways. First, we will remove the present sleeping state, and in the course of events, start removing past sleeping states.

We will begin the repair of the past, going much further than just the life of the machine. We will start repairing the electrical field of the essential self which goes back a very long way—farther back even than the time-space continuum.

Everything is an electrical field; everything is made of electricity. The electrical field of the essential self and of the machine impinge one upon the other. Both of these are within a larger electrical field called *biological life*—itself within a larger electrical field called the time-space continuum, which exists within a still larger field which is so far beyond electrical events that it exists only as a pure, extremely complex mathematical equation—built out of very simple units or building blocks, which in their raw native state are totally undifferentiated, forming a more or less endless ocean of light in infinite extension.

The equation which is the primal but totally potential cause of all phenomena is held in place by sheer force of will, and is shattered intentionally by smaller sub-equations, expressed as sound, which causes the light to devolve into electrical phenomena. We will talk about this in detail later on.

The essential self exists within and slightly outside the electrical field of the machine. It interpenetrates the electrical field of the machine. Each interpenetrates the other, and they affect one another. Each borrows from the other.

The electrical field of the essential self tends to seek a certain electrical field for which it has affinity called the *field affinity*.

The essential self tends to gravitate toward that machine for which it has the most affinity, and thus tends to repeat the

188

same experiential lifetime. It is as if it falls toward the hole that it fits exactly, like a key which falls into the lock.

Even when the machine is in the waking state, this affinity continues. Only by actually changing the electrical field through the process of transformation can we change our destiny, or *karma*—by which is meant our tendency to fall into that particular field for which we have the most affinity.

Eventually, as transformation occurs, the electrical field of the essential self changes. This modification of the electrical field of the essential self which frees it from the affinity-attraction to the machine is the specific and technical definition of the word *transformation*.

Specific changes in the electrical field of the essential self, made with exact knowledge, free it from the affinity factors by which it is drawn into involvement with lower electrical fields in the lower dimensions.

As the electrical field of the essential self is changed, transformed, it loses affinity for the machine, for its corresponding negative electrical field, and for the lower dimensions in general.

If we have made the correct modifications in the electrical field of the essential self, it begins to seek the static potential of the higher-dimensional field.

No matter what changes we make in the machine as a transformational apparatus, its field will still remain an affinity-attraction for *something*. It has a specific *valence* in the chemical-electrical sense.

Chemical valence is nothing new or mysterious. It is used in chemistry to indicate the number of electrons which form an electrical hole into which a positively charged particle will want to fall—*want* to, in the mathematical sense of inevitability-by-probability.

A positively charged convex particle "wants" to be attracted into a negative pocket—what could be called a concave electrical hole in the general field.

This is sex in the highest mathematical abstract, being drawn into intimacy and involvement because two fields just happen to be matched positive to negative, convex to concave.

Several things are operating here: similarity of picture, similarity of emotional content or emotional significance, similarity of intellectual or mental significance, similarity by particularity—in the sense of a seemingly similar smell, sight, or color—a perceptual similarity.

Then there is similarity by charge, by whole chains of charge going back for years, even centuries and more...seeming similarity by shape, content and intensity of an electrical anomaly. The brain sees by comparison, learns by comparison, and orients itself by comparison.

We are suggestible in the sense that one thing which seems similar to something else suggests that we include both in a fusion of synthesis, and categorize them together to save storage space in the memory sectors.

We don't think about this automatic comparative process; it doesn't happen with our awareness. It is not an intellectual process which occurs.

The similarity is suggested so rapidly that without our perceptual awareness, millions or billions or even trillions of similar events can get pulled into impingement, causing a permanent distortion of that electrical event. Permanent, that is, unless we have a way of going back to it and clearing it away.

This can happen dozens, or hundreds, or even thousands of times in one single event. Bursts of impingement are brought in by suggestion. That suggestion is electrical in nature. And the suggestion is in a perceptual suggestion; it is so rapid that it happens far below our level of awareness.

We may know something happened. We may feel the effect of the field distortion, but we don't know specifically what happened until we look at the event, examine it, magnify it and start combing it electrically for charge. Then we can see what we did, what we unconsciously brought in on ourselves by suggestion.

We will find that not only did the machine bring its own comparatives in, but it borrowed from the essential self's electrical field; it tapped its own storage bank, and then, not satisfied with that, it tapped the storage sectors of the essential self's electrical field as well, confusing the issue with events that happened when the essential self wasn't even vaguely human. It is easy to imagine what kind of distortions *that* would produce on the machine's electrical field.

Let's call the essential self "A" disk. It has the basic programs with which it processes information and with which it experiences some sort of passage through the larger electrical field which we call the time-space continuum.

In addition to this, it also has its own memory stored as itself. The essential self *is* its own self-memory in the sense that memory is stored electrically in a specific shape, in this case, expressed as an individuum, having self-knowledge and a sense of personal existence, and occupying a definite place in the mathematical equation which contains all subsets and variables, of which the essential self happens to be a part.

Memory of specific events are actually distortions within the field. We don't want to erase the entire memory, but instead, clear the impingements which have caused matrix distortions, patterns which make some parts of memory inaccessible and even painful.

We want to rehabilitate the memory because bugs have crept into the "A" disk, into the essential self's memory sectors as a result of its encounters with various external field distortions producing internal field distortions.

What would we call it when something starts to happen, when memory starts to fail? Bad sectors? System crash? Some people's experience of themselves can be described as a system crash.

We can see a system's crash when somebody is totally caved in. We can see somebody who has bad memory sectors, areas of their own electrical fields which they would rather not return to, look at, or access. Nobody wants to encounter or re-stimulate bad sectors.

"B" disk is the experiential memory of the machine plus whatever the machine has borrowed from the essential self and from other machines in the way of self-programming and conditioning. If we take the basic program of the "A" disk away, the "B" disk is nothing. It has no being; it has nothing of itself.

It borrows from the "A" disk the memory and programs of the essential self for its very existence, for its life, for its self-awareness. It isn't even self-aware with the "A" disk to impose awareness upon it.

A machine cannot possibly be self-aware. It borrows its self-awareness from the essential self. It is filled with the essential self.

And for this reason, it doesn't want the essential self to ever go away; when it does, it knows that it will lose its sense of self-awareness, of fulfillment, of being full with life, of being full with presence. It doesn't want to lose its visitor. It doesn't want it to go away or to leave it. Once it has been penetrated, it wants to remain penetrated.

So it has the urge to seduce the essential self into itself. It seduces mathematically and electrically, and *when this seduction is answered by the essential self, the resulting compulsive affinity-attraction can be described as a malfunctioning of the essential self, indicating the remedy of transformation.*

This force of affinity is based not on the associative mind or the associative emotions, but on analogies or similarities of wave patterns of light, sound and electricity.

Before transformation, the essential self *likes* biological affinity-structures and doesn't care how this is satisfied. It responds to the machine as the machine in turn responds to stimulation of the pleasure-center.

Identification with the machine satisfies a certain electrical craving, a pleasure center craving which has become an aberration of the essential self.

The closer the affinity between the essential self and the machine, the more the craving is reduced...there is less interference wave. A beat frequency oscillation is reduced, so the pain of craving is diminished.

Pain can express itself as yearning or as a craving. It actually seems like a craving for a certain kind of pleasure or fulfillment, but actually it is a reduction or a subsiding of the dissimilarity, the field dissonance, which is satisfied by intimacy.

Of course, if the essential self had not been drawn into the machine, transformation and evolution would be impossible, so although it occurred by accident, we can take it as serendipitous, a fortunate accident which gives us an opportunity we would not have had otherwise.

Remember that the machine has a powerful and active will, although it is not real will. The machine's will is mechanical and fixated, and so also the machine's attraction for the essential self is electrically seductive. But the essential self also has the capability of using seduction as a tool.

The two seductions that it uses are its only real ability of will. These two real powers—the will of presence, which simply means the will to be present in the present, and the will of attention which means the will to place and fixate the attention on an object, whether tangible, solid or abstract, concentrated or dissipated—are seductive in the sense that their application forces the machine to respond reflexively with the waking state in much the same way that the motor centrum of the machine would respond to the stimulation of lovemaking.

The essential self can apply still another seductive force to add to the force of these two real powers. This added force is called *adoration*. Adoration is the only genuine emotion which the essential self has developed prior to transformation.

With the proper training, we can learn to determine whether we have successfully activated the will of attention, will of presence, or the force of adoration.

We can see whether the machine is active or passive, and whether the essential self is active or passive in relation to the machine.

We can also determine the exact degree of impingement of the two fields. The more active the electrical field of the machine, the more we say the sleep state is active. The less active it is, the more the waking state has been achieved, and the more the essential self's electrical field will be revealed.

Our awareness cannot obtain information on the electrical field and electrical events without associative pictures. We cannot grasp the field with our ordinary awareness, but we are aware of pictures, feelings, sensations, and thoughts within ourselves, and we do follow our inner dialogue in which we draw constantly changing conclusions about everything in our experience.

We are aware of our mental pictures, the significance we give them, our considerations, our emotions, or at least, of how the emotions make us feel. We are aware of our sensations which are produced by the emotions—by their impingement upon the mental field.

If we do happen to become aware of our own electrical field, we will notice a definite electrical flow occurring in a specific pattern. We may think of ourselves in this sense as a swarm of tiny bees in which each bee seems powerfully charged with an electrical field of its own.

This is our first intimation of real consciousness. We have become *aware* of ourselves; we have *known ourselves* for a moment or two. If we think about it, we realize we are just an electrical field within an electrical field impinging upon an electrical field for which we happen to have affinity. And what is the machine in the mathematical sense? A nothingness, a hole into which we fell, and in which we remained, and will remain, because it will never decay naturally and dissipate itself into the larger electrical field of which it is an immortal part.

It is our opposite number, our soul mate, our ideal partner, and unless we do something about it, we have gotten together forever. We have fallen into a black hole, and until something seriously changes, we are going to stay in that black hole, recurring around and around its centrum of gravity.

Now what can an electrical field do about this situation? Transformation, we know, reduces the affinity between the essential self and the machine. The reduction of affinity should therefore only occur after the machine has served its function as a transformational apparatus.

If nothing else happened, the machine and its essential self would never be attracted to a school, but under certain conditions, they are attracted by the same force of affinity which brought the essential self and the machine together in the first place.

A school is not just a place where people gather to learn something new with the mental apparatus. A real school is actually an anomaly—a very unusual displacement of energy —in the larger electrical field.

It produces affinity for the essential self's field, plus the machine's field. By accident or design—usually the result of some deliberate interference by a member of a school during the early formative years, which could be only a momentary encounter—the combined field of the machine and the essential self develop an affinity for a school.

The field of the school will never change. At a certain point, our affinity for the school will reduce and we will leave.

Either the essential self has achieved its transformation, in which case it no longer needs a school, or the combined field of the essential self and the machine return to the ordinary state, in which case it has no more affinity for the school than billions of other similar fields. It either goes away because it has evolved, or it goes away because it has devolved.

In this sense we have no more control over our presence in a school than about our utterly involuntary presence in the machine. People who leave a school don't remember the school. They don't know why they were there. It is as if that part of their memory was erased. They returned to ordinary life and became ordinary again. Their reason for being in the school is no longer evident to them.

Two things may have happened. The essential self evolved out of the machine, and, in this case, the machine returns to ordinary life empty, and has no memory of the school. The essential selves have succeeded in transformation, but not the Work, leaving them free from the machine, which has returned to ordinary life.

In a sense, these people are dead, empty. You can see it in their eyes. There is no one home. They have little or no memory of ever having been in a school, and no discernible purpose for having been in a school. Or, they failed to accomplish what they set out to do, in which case, a degeneration occurs, and the essential self and the machine both return to ordinary life; they will have very good memory, but a sense of failure and anger—self-loathing.

Sometimes we may see the same model returning with a different customer. Some empties just hang around the school for years out of sheer habit.

In the ordinary world this is very evident in the university system. People go to college and then just remain around the college by sheer momentum, many years after graduation.

The memory of having been in a school belongs to the essential self, and when the essential self rises out of the machine, the machine has little or no memory of actual events which occurred while it was in the school, although it may vaguely recall having somehow—it can't quite recall how or why—been a part of the school.

And of course this happens quite naturally. After all, the machine has only a machine's memory, and it is able to remember everything very clearly, that is, right up to the time it went into the school, and then it remembers everything afterwards, but it has selective amnesia about things that happened during its time in a school.

It won't have a sense of failure, just mild bewilderment. It can't imagine what it was every doing in a school. This is most evident in a machine which has been vacated by the essential self.

In another case, the essential self eventually gives up the struggle, subsides, and lives out the rest of its existence in the machine. This is a very pitiful situation. Even though there is good memory—and even fond memory—of the school, and the individual may keep up his or her relationship with the school, he or she has failed and is painfully aware of it.

There is a third case. The essential self has achieved transformation and entered the Work, in which case, the machine and the essential self have become one; the affinity of the machine and the essential self has been eliminated by the elimination of both parties, forming a third party which has a new affinity for something much higher.

In this case, we steal the machine for the Work; nobody misses it; the machine simply remains out of the mainstream of life. We remove very few such machines, and statistically our activities are not noticeable by nature, and nature does not respond with its crushing revenge.

If the essential self is transformed to the degree that it enters the Work, the machine and the essential self are one and the same—the two become one. A secondary transformation occurs when one enters the Work in which the machine is transformed as a new kind of transformational apparatus.

Thus, we see three distinct cases: in the first case, a total failure, a complete crash has occurred; the machine remains as it was and the essential self remains as it was. They both just go away, and it's back to business as usual.

In the second case, the essential self has evolved somewhat, leaving the empty machine to return to its usual routine. The essential self is no longer drawn into that particular machine, but because it is not entirely free, it is eventually drawn into something—but something much higher—in which there may or may not be an opportunity for further transformation.

Sometimes going into a higher dimension can be a dead end in itself, because from there opportunities might not present themselves.

In the third case, a mutually reciprocal initiation and

transformation occurs in which the essential self does not go too far beyond the machine, and the machine is brought along in a mutually spiraling reciprocal initiation toward transformation, so that for all practical purposes, eventually, the two electrical fields become so similar that there is no difference between the essential self and the machine.

It isn't possible to enter the Work without a machine which has been transformed, and at the same time, preparation for the Work provides the necessity for transformation and places us in a situation in which transformation is an inevitable necessity.

Ultimately, our own essential annihilation in the process of transformation can be turned back toward the machine, all along the way.

This is reflected in the mystical poetry of the lover and the beloved. As each of them takes a step on the ladder, they turn to help the other in a mutually reciprocal process of initiation. You help me, I help you. This is expressed in the ancient folk-saying, "one hand washes the other."

We can, if we wish, leave the machine and enter into a relationship with a much higher individuum by freeing ourselves from the seduction of the machine's electrical field, which would amount to getting ourselves out of one hole and into another hole, a more pleasant hole, a more exalted hole, but still a hole.

The alternative to that is to work with what we have right now. We can use our present situation to prepare for and get ourselves accepted into the Work.

We may want to give it all up and reach for something more exalted, but there is no guarantee that we will get into the Work with something more exalted any more than we would with what we have now.

The chances are, in fact, far less because we may dead end into a situation so exalted and so profoundly unchangeable that from it, there is no escape.

The best possible scenario in this event is that the essential self would actually continue to evolve, but there are no guarantees; it might do better or it might do worse than in the present situation. Nothing is certain about this.

We don't know where the better chance for getting into the Work lies. In a sense, though, we do know what the odds are. If we make an evolutionary mistake somewhere along the line, if we forget the needs of the machine to evolve with us, if we leave the machine behind because we have taken two steps on the ladder instead of one, then we have no choice but to seek something higher, because our relationship with the machine will be automatically severed.

We will find ourselves in a situation in which we are forced to seek a more exalted individuum with which to enter the Work, and in the meantime, in the human world, we'll return the empty bottles. This shows a clear lack of consideration for our work partner and indicates an unreadiness to enter the Work in any case.

If we become impatient with ourselves, with the machine, with the situation, or with our lack of progress, we may decide to take two rungs at a time, even though we are well aware that the machine can't possibly keep up with us.

Our first taste of real freedom can easily seduce us away from the concept of divine slavery, by which I mean an intentional working partnership with the machine.

We must not forget that the machine is an empty hole in the electrical field into which we have fallen. It is a place we occupy, not a thing in itself.

When a machine comes to a school, we have in a sense moved a hole from its rightful place, its ordinary destiny. We could easily become so excited about our temporary release from our ordinary destiny—and rest assured that it *is* only temporary, a sanctuary provided by the school for the purpose of giving someone the freedom to work toward preparation for the Work—that we ultimately might be tempted to escape and so lose our place in the Work, because the life of the machine *is* our rightful place in the Work, if we accept the challenge.

Then we must find another potential place in the Work, another machine, and hopefully, eventually be attracted to a school again, under certain conditions.

Of course it may happen that the new machine never achieves those conditions or a school may not be available at that time. There are only so many who can be in a school at any given moment. We are under a set of very inflexible and inexorable electrical laws in a school.

Attraction to a school does not occur by interest, information or accident, but by electrical affinity. Without affinity for a school, one cannot possibly enter a school.

E.J. Gold, All In One, Charcoal on Rives BFK, 1987

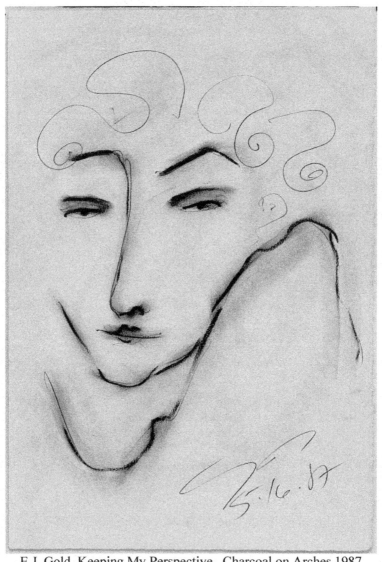

E.J. Gold, Keeping My Perspective , Charcoal on Arches 1987

CHAPTER 21

The Restimulation of the Defense Mechanism

By constantly restimulating areas of charge in the electrical field of the machine, we are able to clear it of its ridges and eddies which impinge on the electrical field of the essential self.

If we understand how the defense mechanism operates and how it defends the machine against the waking state, then we can have at least some working idea of what it means to deliberately stimulate and restimulate the chronic—the machine's defense mechanism against the waking state.

In order to understand how the chronic is intentionally restimulated in a school, we must remember very clearly that the defense mechanism which we call the chronic is a system of conditioning which keeps a machine—which is in fact a five-level electrical field—in the sleeping state.

205

The essential self does not have an electrical field—it is an electrical field...an electrical field which is oppositely charged from the machine's electrical field, both of which have reciprocal wave form patterns in relation to each other.

It is also important to remember that the machine is not actually a thing or an object, but an absence in the greater electrical field which we call *organic life*.

The machine is a tube-like electrical field which exhibits very specific variations along its length, which we represent to ourselves as the process of birth, life and death in organic matter. But this is just a way of explaining to ourselves something which is happening on an electrical level.

We tend to impose biological life significance upon electrical phenomena, but the fact is that we are viewing a blue-gray electrical field generated by sound—and even that is just a simple way of looking at it.

The field has no color other than the color we assign to it. We assign color in the first place because it helps us to differentiate between the refractive and reflexive index of one or another sub-field of electrical phenomena.

We do so because for one reason or another, we happen to be able to discern the subtractive effect of an electrical field upon light which happens to fall within the noticeable range of the electro-magnetic spectrum.

The electrical field of the machine exists as a single event. It doesn't start to exist at conception and end its existence at the degeneration of the body—either through decomposition in the ground or through highly accelerated oxidation in a crematorium—contemporary human beings' answer to real estate shortages.

The machine exists as a single unit throughout its entire existence. We tend to view cross sections of it in a linear way, which gives the distinct impression that the machine begins its existence at one point and ends its existence at another point, but actually we are looking at it sideways, as if we were looking at a cross section of a steel bar.

Suppose we examine the idea of a steel bar which is five feet long and one inch thick. We'll imagine looking at it broadside in front of us, holding one end with one hand, the other end with the other hand. In this view, it looks like a single object with neither beginning nor end except as it exists or doesn't exist.

Now suppose we turned the bar end-on and entered it from one end. In this view, we would see it in cross section, and imagine that we were able to somehow travel from one end of the bar to the other end of the bar, and that it seemed to us that the subjective impression of this passage changed continually in very subtle ways, which we might call the passage of time.

It would seem as if we had just begun existing when we first entered it at one end, and that we stopped existing when we passed out the other end.

The machine is just exactly like that. It is something that we are looking at from one end to the other from inside it, one cross section at a time. We are travelling through it sideways.

That is not the way that the objective time flow happens. We are travelling across time, not through it. We are taking a right angle cross section through the time flow which we call subjective time.

Objective time is occurring at right angles to the time that we ordinarily seem to perceive. So we might imagine this iron rod with another iron rod, then another one, and so on, laid down side-by-side, off into the farthest distance.

Then we take a cross section of one, then the next and the next.

It would give us the impression that we were experiencing the same thing over and over again, when in fact, we aren't. Although it is very similar, the differences are subtle, almost unnoticeable, and the differences don't become evident for millions and millions of passes. From one pass to the next, there doesn't appear to be much change.

If the machine were in the waking state, we would experience the entire iron bar as a whole picture and begin to move through time. We would begin taking forward motion through time at right angles to the time that we normally experience.

Momentarily we take a breathless step out of time and space—a split-second in the eternal moment—and it seems as if everything is standing still, because the movement that we ordinarily perceive is movement of a cross section. Here's the entire rod, and we are travelling sideways in relation to how we were just travelling before. Nothing is moving, nothing is happening, there is no time flow.

Somewhere along the line we will re-enter the same lifetime; we will pick up the scan at the same place, except that we will be maybe three or four million iron rods down the line, but we won't realize it, because each one is exactly the same as the other one except for the fact that it is down the line.

Eventually we will be concerned with the actual inner workings of the defense mechanism and later on with

208

disarming the defense mechanism.

We could view the disarming of the defense mechanism as dismantling a dangerous and volatile bomb, in which we must find a way to slip behind the triggers.

The defense mechanism is like a bomb that is about to go off at any given moment. And what is it exactly that sets off the defense mechanism? The approach—the threat—of the waking state, turns on the defense mechanism, which then conveys us safely away from it.

If we were to accidentally wander into a movie studio or a music recording studio, a security guard would come along and gently guide us out of the area.

The function of the defense mechanism is to convey us out of the Forbidden Zone—the waking state. Depending upon how rapidly we entered this Forbidden Zone, the defense mechanism will be more or less urgent about conveying us back to the sleep state.

The defense mechanism will be extremely courteous if we just happen to wander a little bit toward the waking state. If we are sleepwalking, it is understandable that we will sometimes drift toward the waking state in spite of ourselves.

The defense mechanism in this case isn't very active; it is rather calm and it comes and takes us by the hand, puts an arm around our shoulder, and moves us gently away in a very calm orderly fashion from the Forbidden Zone.

But, let's say that a shock happens to occur and we are suddenly propelled almost through the Forbidden Zone into the waking state.

We have crossed the neutral zone and we are at this

moment in forbidden territory.

It's as if a Russian submarine happened to be fourteen miles off the Pacific coast. It would just be waved off, and nobody would be particularly bothered. But, let's say there was a Russian submarine in the Hudson River. The reaction would tend to be a little more intense—one might consider for example a small, tactical thermo-nuclear response over Kiev.

A sudden shock can propel the machine into the waking state...or near the waking state. If that happens, the defense mechanism will tend to be more severe or more violent. Now just imagine it as a security guard, and the reaction of a security guard when we wander past the front gate of the Pentagon as opposed to the same security guard's reaction if he suddenly found us in the War Room.

The defense mechanism could go so far as to produce death as an answer to the waking state. It is not very likely, but it could. It certainly can produce extreme nausea, anxiety, severe upset, anger, hysteria, and so on.

As soon as we begin dramatizing the defense mechanism, the machine enters the sleeping state, and once again, everything is nice and quiet.

The dramatization will produce the sleeping state in the machine if it has wandered too close to the waking state.

What happens is that electricity courses through; we can feel it coursing through us when we get angry and start dramatizing the anger. If we feel the anger, we will notice a profound electrical effect occurring throughout the machine. It crackles with electricity. At that point, the defense mechanism has come into play and has taken the machine away from the waking state.

210

It would not do any good to just ram our machine into the waking state because the defense mechanism will trigger, the security guards will come. There is no way to brazenly walk into the waking state without attracting the attention of a security guard—the defense mechanism.

We have got to find a way to get into the waking state without triggering the defense mechanism, to get past the security guard. We will do this in a variety of ways which we call the Keys. But eventually we are going to outgrow the use of Keys. It won't be enough just to use the Keys to bypass the security guard.

At some point, we are going to dismantle the defense mechanism itself, leaving just enough defense mechanism that we don't wander accidentally from the sleeping state into the waking state, but if we want to, we can pass the security guard very easily.

The defense mechanism is composed of a few hundred components parts—not a particularly complex structure—each part of which is made from a very simple component assembled in much the same way as DNA protein chains. It is the electrical counterpart to DNA.

Eventually we will disassemble the defense mechanism entirely, like disassembling a bomb. But before we can disassemble a time bomb, we have got to disassemble or bypass the triggering mechanism itself. In order to gain access to the triggering mechanism, we must use something akin to jumper cables.

After we dismantle the defense mechanism, we will find ourselves in a direct confrontation with a very different level of problems and solutions than we've been used to. At first, we address problems and solutions of the sleeping state and of the machine and its relationship to its environment.

In the lower levels of this work we will remain occupied with the machine's sleeping state. We can't expect anything other than this personal and environmental preoccupation in our present condition.

We should not be surprised if we happen to occasionally enter the waking state as a result of our beginning work efforts, but at the same time, we should not be surprised if a few moments later the sleeping state reasserts itself. This is completely natural in the early stages of work.

Even as we reach higher levels of work, the sleeping state will naggingly continue to reassert itself. No need to worry, in fact, we want the sleeping state to work for us. We can use both sleeping and waking states equally well for our work.

The sleeping state is as valuable to a serious worker as the waking state. It has its own uses. So to begin with, we are going to attempt to find a way to deal with problems of the sleeping state and find solutions to those problems while allowing the machine to remain natural and relaxed in the sleeping state.

Then comes the transition period, after which we enter a more or less permanent waking state punctuated by sleep and play, both necessary forms of rest and relaxation of the tensions of the waking state.

Most of the problems of the waking state result from the inevitable phantom reverberations from the sleeping state which continue to persist.

It is behaving as if in the sleeping state, yet it is in the waking state.

At this point, we now turn back to a lower level of work and review some of the earlier material, but this time we do it in the waking state. Now the same exercises that produced sleeping state problems and solutions before, suddenly produce entirely different reactions and totally different results.

We are not really going back over the same thing. We are doing two differrent exercises that have the same wording, that ask us to address the same questions, yet address totally different areas.

We will scan to see if the sleeping state still has hooks, to see if there is anything left on machine levels.

E.J. Gold, A Friend of Silence , Charcoal on Arches 1987

CHAPTER 22

Every Which Way But Up

The quest for the permanent vision of the higher dimension may strike us as odd, but we must understand how the vision of another world—even without knowing much about it—would change us and bring about our certain transformation.

The reflex effect upon the machine, automatically produced by the not automatically produced vision of the higher dimension, not automatic in the sense that a definite effort is required to produce and maintain this vision, will result in the definite arousing of certain unusual sensations which should, in turn, provoke the waking state.

Any shock of a particular nature will produce the waking state; however, the waking state by itself is not enough. The waking state is necessary, yet, at the same time, one must be able to actually view the higher dimensions. Using the

215

machine in the waking state in relation to the higher dimensions is what activates its transformational qualities.

Without the vision of the higher dimension, we might as well sit and do nothing, basking in the waking state as with any other momentary sensation of pleasure.

The waking state inevitably produces the vision of the higher dimensions, although we may not know that this is what we are looking at. In turn, the vision of the higher dimensions correspondingly produces the waking state. One does not exist without the other.

But at the same time, unless we know that we are viewing the higher dimensions, we cannot function in the higher dimensions, and will continue to function as if in the lower dimension and the sleeping state.

The waking state is not particularly difficult to achieve. It is achieved many times during the course of the average day except that we don't ordinarily have our attention set to catch those times. Your machine might even be in the waking state at this very moment. Normally the momentum of our prior activities carries us through the waking state and, before we realize it, the waking state is gone.

We need not think of this vision in the mystical or shamanistic sense. It's no more of a mystical vision than what we see all day every day. What differs is our way of operating with what we see. When we see the higher dimensions, the difference is in the detail.

Rather than seeing the brain's holographic representation of the world, we will be looking at the world itself. Ordinarily, we look at the brain's three-dimensional tactile hallucinations projected within itself in holographic form.

216

But because the brain is limited to a specific and very finite number of alterable holographic symbol units, the amount of perceivable detail is always subjectively the same. Details are eliminated as necessary to accommodate the brain's inherent limits. When we bypass the brain's inner holographic projection of the world, we perceive it directly. When the human biological machine goes transparent, we look directly at the environment. We see it with all the detail that the environment has.

When the detail improves, the color improves, the sounds improve, all the perceptual qualities, the texture of the environment, the texture of our reality changes radically, but if we see a table in front of us, we will still see the table there; it's not going to turn into something like a huge lemon or a paisley couch. It's still going to be a table, only more so.

We will be able to perceive the detail of the entire room as if we were looking at one thing and yet we had our attention concentrated on a single object; our attention will expand to include the entire field of vision, rather than becoming diffused and scattered.

The waking state is produced by something-or-other, but even if we don't quite know what, we do know that in the waking state the barrier to the perception of the higher dimensions is removed. So all we need to do is perceive the higher dimension in order to bring the machine into the waking state.

Obtaining the vision of the higher dimension is an indication that the waking state has been achieved, and at the same time, without the vision of the higher dimension, the waking state can't be utilized for transformation.

Two electrical fields impinging upon one another produce a variety of effects. One effect can be that the dominant field can often alter the subordinate field. In this case, the essential self is the subordinate field.

It doesn't have very much will over the machine, but it does have the will of attention, so its principal tool is attention, and its secondary tool is presence. We can only use those two things. Attention is the most powerful tool we can use to produce the shock which brings the human biological machine into the waking state.

There are a variety of ways in which we can use attention to produce the shock to bring the machine into the waking state, which in turn produces the transformational effect upon the essential self.

The various ideas that we may have, things that we try, often do not work, and the reason that they do not work is specifically because they don't produce the buildup of electrical energy, although they may produce a mild shock. If shock itself did it, skydiving would work to produce the waking state, but it doesn't.

There's a state of exhilaration which is a false waking state. It's so close to the real waking state that it's almost undetectably different. However, there is a definite difference between the state of exhilaration and the waking state of the machine.

A good technique will take into account that there is a false waking state—a state of exhilaration, and/or ecstasy, and, by taking that into account, will produce the waking state without touching those things which produce the state of exhilaration or ecstasy or both. In other words, good technique does not

218

produce exhilaration, but it does produce the waking state.

We can produce one thing which is right next to something else. For instance, we can precipitate strontium 90 which looks like calcium, because the two are chemically the same, except that they are internally different. Strontium 90 and calcium are interchangeable in chemical combination, although they are completely different chemicals. They behave similarly. So if we were trying to isolate strontium 90, we would have to isolate it from calcium.

In the same way, we must learn to differentiate between the waking state and the sleeping state of the machine...remembering that it's the machine which is in a waking or sleeping state and not the essential self, and that the essential self does not wake or sleep. It has simple presence and is neither awake nor asleep.

The only reason the essential self seems to be asleep is because it identifies with the sleeping state of the machine. It falls into the sleeping state of the machine. Because the machine is in the sleeping state, the essential self is convinced that it also is in the sleeping state. This is the correct definition of identification.

Identification is not bad in itself; in fact, it's a wonderful tool if it's used right. But if identification produces the definite impression that one is asleep because the machine is asleep, then identification is harmful rather than useful.

In the waking state, the machine is not really there for all practical purposes. It doesn't exert its will, so there's no difference between the essential self and the machine. In the waking state, the machine and the essential self are one; they are identical.

In the sleeping state, electrical anomalies in the machine's field produce various forms of pain and unconsciousness.

Of course, as we put our attention on the machine and on the possibility of sleep, we know that the machine will awaken slightly. And if we can remember that the machine is in the sleeping state, we can be more alert to the potential for its awakening; and, when we notice something different we can ask ourselves "Is this the waking state?"

It may or may not be. But just asking ourselves if it is the waking state means that we are alert to the possibility.

It's extremely unlikely that we would recognize the waking state in the course of ordinary life. And it is very rare that we would find ourselves in a situation where we suddenly look up, and say, "Hey, the machine's in the waking state right now!"

The chances are that the momentum of activity will carry the vestigial effects of the sleeping state through the waking state. The sheer momentum of our daily activity will probably impose the sleeping state effects even when the machine is awake.

So we don't often recognize that the machine is in the waking state simply because we are continuing to carry on as if the machine were asleep. The machine is not imposing its will, but out of sheer habit and momentum, we continue to carry on as if the machine were still imposing its will upon us.

So a method is necessary to ensure that when the machine does enter the waking state, it does not carry forward out of momentum those habitual sleeping state manifestations and effects which mask the waking state in the course of ordinary life.

This method is highly technical. It requires some skill; it requires some artistry. But it is possible for anyone who is seriously interested to learn it within six months to a year.

But within the matter of a month or two we can achieve the waking state more occasionally than not. In other words, fairly often...four or five times a week, maybe even more. We should be able to achieve the waking state on our own volition, our own power.

We can't do anything without the waking state. At the same time, once the waking state has been achieved, our work has just begun.

The use of the waking state gives us the opportunity to test this teaching in the sense that if we can achieve the waking state under our own power, if we can produce the waking state n our own machine, from that moment on, we will never doubt what is coming. We will never doubt the rest of it.

In other words, right now this is just a theory, an interesting idea—if it works. When we *actually* produce the waking state in our own machine for the very first time—we will be absolutely convinced of its reality. From that point on, we don't need any convincing, all we need to do is work.

It's just a matter of work effort and we are going to spend years achieving this. It's not something that happens over night, but in each stage along the way, we will have adequate demonstration that what we are working on is a reality. Not many methods offer demonstrations and proofs along the way.

In some people, the waking state is spontaneously produced quite often. In most people, however, it is not.

We will not even necessarily recognize that we are

receiving information from a higher dimension, because we don't really have the tools for recognition. We would be most unwise to trust it till we understand what it actually is.

We don't *need* anything from the higher dimension in order to accomplish our transformation. It's just not necessary. It's an interesting sidelight, but not something we are actually going to require. And it is not conclusive. We have no way of knowing what comes from a higher dimension in relation to our dimension. Unless we can see into the higher dimension and know what it is—then we have a reference for it.

At that point, we recognize it as something from a higher dimension only if we recognize from which higher dimension it came and what part it plays in the higher dimension.

In terms of working alone or in a group situation, it depends on how fast we want to work. If we want to work individually and spend say thirty years achieving enough of a waking state that we can begin work, then by all means we should work by ourselves. But if we prefer to work a lot faster and achieve in two weeks what normally would take five or six years to accomplish, then we might decide that we prefer to work in a group.

E.J. Gold, Watching Over My Shoulder, Charcoal on Sennelier, 1989

E.J. Gold, Grinding Halt , Charcoal on Arches 1990

CHAPTER 23

An Experience

The following is an account of an experience which Janet, a medical doctor located in New York City, had with her chronic and how she was able to use it to cross into the waking state.

"It was very late at night and I was working in the intensive care unit. The ICU, as we call it, is a very high pressure ward. I was exhausted and all I wanted to do was go to sleep, but I couldn't, I had to follow one of my patients very closely if I didn't want to lose him.

"I kept hoping I would be able to rest for a few minutes but it was impossible. I couldn't take a break and lie down for a while, I just had to keep going.

"At one point, it was necessary to have a lab test done immediately. It was a question of life or death. I was really concerned with this patient. But I was so exhausted, all I wanted to do was go to sleep. So I became annoyed that I

225

couldn't get any rest. My chronic just came right up and I got very angry.

"I already knew from prior observation that my personal chronic was anger, so I was particularly surprised to see it once again. Anyway, I got angry, sharp and crisp as I usually do when my chronic is active.

"I took a blood sample and brought it over to an orderly and asked him to bring it to the lab for me and have the test run. The test takes about forty-five seconds all together. The orderly refused to bring the sample to the lab because of Union rights. You can imagine how that fired my chronic! I was furious!

"I went to the lab myself and when I got there, the technician wasn't in the lab to run my blood right away. So I had to do it myself. I was seething! My chronic was in full operation.

"All of a sudden I caught my reflection in a little mirror hanging on the wall. I just happened to turn around and there I was face to face with my chronic. I saw my chronic fully operating. What a shock! That was it. Everything went boom and I was suddenly awake. My anger was gone.

"The room changed slightly. It wasn't freaky and farout like it has been or could be. It was just what it was for that moment.

"But I knew. I absolutely knew that my machine was in the waking state and that this occurred in relation to the operation of my chronic. I understood in what way I could use my chronic to achieve the waking state. I knew how it worked and I knew that if I could use my chronic more often in that way, then I could achieve the waking state more often.

226

"Now I know that the state I was in is the last step, the only thing that is in my way to the waking state. I know that that is my protection device, the thing that is protecting me from the waking state. For some reason at that moment there was no danger from my entering the waking state, so I was able to make that transition. I can't tell why. At that moment I could, at other times I can't.

"Maybe the reason that it happened to me is because I was aware of myself in that moment and I was provided with the shock of seeing my chronic in the mirror. It was as if some sort of strange alien mask had affixed itself over my face.

"The point is that maybe there is a way that we can provide a shock for ourselves at the point at which we can really be observing ourselves and know we are just about there. I know that I am not always going to be that lucky, to have a mirror handy just at that moment. In fact, I know that mirror won't work a second time.

"But we shouldn't have to depend on accidental shock. There must be something that we can intentionally do, if we are aware enough to know that we are near the waking state.

"I am not quite sure what happened between the state in which my chronic was operating and the state where suddenly my machine was awake. I am not sure I can define what happened that made the change. But I'll tell you what I think happened.

"In a sense these circumstances were probably ideal conditions. The shock happened to be accidental at that particular time, in that particular instance; the shock was the transition factor but we should not have to depend upon an accidental shock.

"The thing that made the difference was that as a result of being aware of my chronic and using the presence techniques that I have learned over the last year from working with G.'s books, when I get to the point where I start getting angry—because that is my chronic—I become aware of the fact that my chronic is active and I remember to observe the machine under the spell of the chronic. I didn't have the word 'chronic' for it before; before I was just being present. Now I can say I observe the force of the chronic upon the machine.

"When I walked into the lab I stood there stewing for no reason. A radio was going and nobody was in there. The space was such a mess.

"I was standing there alone knowing I was being angry for no reason. I realized it was my chronic, and then saw my reflection in the mirror. Had I not known at that moment that it was my chronic I was seeing in the mirror, I could have been completely overtaken by my anger. My anger was at the point where I could have just chewed somebody out. I could have called the tech and screamed at him. I could have done a lot of things. I could have repressed it.

"In fact, what I did was I observed it as my chronic and at that moment caught my reflection and saw myself observing my chronic and that is when it went over. That is when it really all transformed.

"I think there is something very important in the fact that I knew it was my chronic. When I thought of it as anger, even though I was in the presence exercise, it didn't work. But as soon as I correctly identified it as the chronic, and identified the chronic as that thing which indicates that my machine is most near the waking state, anything, a mirror or whatever could have served as a shock. It didn't matter what it was.

"I could have seen a suture, or I could have seen a butterfly clamp, or I could have seen a clock, anything could have served to function as a shock mechanism at that point. Anything could have done it. All I had to do was realize that it was the chronic and, because I was seeing the chronic, that I was very near to the waking state. The mirror happened to serve the function of the necessary shock because it showed me my own face under the domination of the chronic.

"To me this is a way of working with signposts that can help us to find the waking state. That might sound ridiculously, stupidly simple, but what other way do we have of find the waking state? After all, we don't know what the waking state is or where it is exactly. We don't have a map. All we know is that it has a name, the waking state. We don't have a map but there are signposts.

"We know how far we are from it and we know how close we are to it by how strongly the chronic is manifesting. It is literally like playing the game of hot and cold. Blind man's bluff where it is said you are getting hotter or colder as you approach or move away from the target object.

"And rather than just seeing if it is hot or cold, we can intentionally put ourselves in the position to make it hotter, which might mean that we a re closer to the waking state. The key to getting really close is to not explode the energy. The hotter you keep it on the inside, the closer you are to the waking state. Anger is my key. This does not mean that I should go out of my way to make myself deliberately angry.

"When the chronic is working, it means that I am bumping into the waking state. Not going into the waking state, not too far away from the waking state, but bumping into it. That is a good picture in my mind. What I have been doing or trying to do since then is to be aware of when my chronic is operating. And I have been able to even allow myself to cross over into the waking state by doing one of two things.

"Number one, certainly not trying to get rid of my chronic, and secondly, not exploding. Not allowing the catharsis. But just by realizing, by the very nature of the fact that I am involved in my chronic, that it means that I am near the waking state, the next step is either to stay where I am or to make the leap. You can just observe it if that's all you want to do. But that is your signpost which says, 'This way to the waking state.'

"That is your absolute key that you are near the waking state. If you can recognize your chronic when it is happening, not try to defend against it, not try to get rid of it, not try to flush it down the toilet, not look at it as something negative, but realize that that is your key to the waking state, then you are getting somewhere.

"We must remember that when our chronic is most powerful then we are at our closest point to the waking state, and when it is less powerful then we are further away. It is almost unnoticeable when we are very far away.

"It stand to reason that a profitable lifestyle would put us in a position where our chronic is perpetually excited. Not a perpetual state of calm where we keep ourselves as far away as possible from the waking state as evidenced by an inactive chronic.

"We must think of ourselves as completely absolutely unable to see our way. We haven't a map and our eyes are closed. The only thing we have is the hot or cold of the chronic. The chronic is a tool which is our worst enemy and our only friend.

"We must search out the situations which most activate the chronic. These are the situations we should be in most of the time, as much as we can tolerate it without making ourselves sick.

"If we can succeed in maintaining ourselves in these stressful situations, then eventually a shock will be provided. We should neither try to explode through nor to pull back. Just stay there and explore, looking for a hole in the fence.

"But there is only really one thing that is necessary. We must understand that nothing is actually instantaneous no matter how instantaneous it may seem to us. There is a cause just prior to something. If my machine enters into the waking state, because it was at the brink, then I can conclude that something sent me over the brink, but that is not important. What brought me to the brink is important. And I should try to get there as often as possible.

"Of course we won't always succeed in going over the brink. What I did was, I allowed my chronic to continue without intervention by observing it, by realizing that it was my chronic.

"But there is something else that I wanted to get across here because I think that most people think that their chronic is something to get rid of. I used to apologize a lot for snapping at people. I used to apologize a lot for being angry. And then all of a sudden I realized that it is my chronic. Not that it is all right to do things to other people, and I try not to, but I cannot express it at people now and allow it to continue, and that is

231

very different. I can allow my chronic to continue its course without acting it out, and without repressing it, and that is when it takes me to the point where in fact I can get to the waking state.

"If you try to repress the feelings because you don't want to act them out or you don't feel that they are right, or you think that there is something wrong with being fearful or angry or frustrated or whatever your chronic happens to be, if you don't stop it from going on its course, it can take you to the point where you can cross over.

"If you start intervening with your intellectualism, if you do anything other than observe it and allow it to be without acting it out, then you lose the opportunity that it affords. With me it is important to not act it out. My chronic is offensive to people, it is not good for me and it may cause a catharsis if I act it out. I don't want this catharsis because it is not going to be helpful to my efforts to achieve the waking state.

"It is just a matter of realizing that your chronic has been activated and allowing it to take you. Like a guide, it will take you by the hand and lead you to the waking state.

"And that is precisely without any question what I did that night. I knew I was being angry. I knew it was because my sleep was being interrupted. I mean all of the reasons that my chronic comes to be and that is when it happened.

"As I was walking around carrying this tube of blood, before it even happened, before it crossed over, I said 'Here I am, boy is my chronic doing it'. And so I started to watch it. I didn't try to stop the feelings. I realized that that was my anger and that is always going to happen to me, at least for the time being and I might as well take a look at it. So I was watching it, but I allowed it to be and I didn't try to stop being angry.

"You are going to try to get rid of the chronic by various means. And one of the ways is to judge it. Another way is to intellectualize it out of existence or to sublimate it and to bring it into a higher plane. You don't want to do that. You want to wallow in the chronic without manifesting the chronic, although if you manifest a little bit, that is fine. Not much though. And let it grab you by the hand. Let it take you to the promised land. The thing you hate most is your guide.

"But the key is to identify it as the chronic. If you think of it as just another state that you are in or if you are totally absorbed in whatever your feelings are and you can only think about them, if you forget that it is the chronic, it will take you nowhere.

"As soon as you correctly identify it as the chronic, it will lead you to and possibly through the barrier. It will actually help you where before it obstructed you, because it is a guidepost. It is a signpost, a definite thing. If you follow it without catharsis, it will lead you directly into the waking state.

"If you go away from it, or reject it, or are oblivious to it, how can it lead you into anything? You have left the path, you see. There is a straight and narrow path. At last I can say I understand the phrase, 'Strait the gate and narrow the way.' "

E.J. Gold, My Friend Pearsall , Charcoal on Arches 1996

Exercise References

Ch 1, "The Situation," Pg. 1

"If we take the time to closely observe a fish tank, we will notice that the tank is a closed environment, a totally independent ecosystem which depends upon a delicate balance of interior equilibrium and interspecies order."

2) Ch. 1, "The Situation," Pg. 3

"Those who live near the surface, such as the goldfish and the redfins, will always be the first served, so they, in a certain sense, dominate the others. Others like the eel will seem perfectly at ease anywhere in the tank—top, middle or bottom."

3) Ch. 2, "What to Do?" Pg. 7

"If the fish were able to build a sandcastle, for example, would it really have accomplished anything of objective significance?"

4) Ch. 2, "What to Do?" Pg. 11

"In addition, he could gather information that would imply that a fixed type and amount of food suddenly appeared in the tank at more or less definite and predictable intervals, and moreover, that other elements of tank maintenance seemed to be in the hands of some unknown agency, acting from above."

5) Ch. 3, "Our Potential for Inner Evolution," Pg. 22

"Let us assume that we know this and, like Redfin, we have had momentary glimpses of the next higher dimension from which we have deduced the existence of an Absolute dimension, and that from this we have further recognized the futility of life in the ordinary sense."

6) Ch. 4, "The Human Biological Machine as a Transformational Apparatus," Pg. 26

"In our beginning work, we will turn our first attention toward the body, with its mental, emotional and motor apparatuses, which when taken as a whole, is called in this system, the human biological machine."

7) Ch. 4, "The Human Biological Machine as a Transformational Apparatus," Pg. 27

"In the sleeping state, its attention is completely fixated on ...which is the real meaning of the ancient myth of Narcissus."

8) Ch. 5, "Beyond Personal Enhancement," Pg. 33

"Even a superficial study of our situation demonstrates clearly that in our present condition, we are utterly powerless to prevent ourselves from being carried along by the machine in these pursuits, the majority of which go completely contrary to our highest aims, aspirations and intentions."

9) Ch. 5, "Beyond Personal Enhancement," Pg. 34

"Although we can come to know and understand the machine in detail, we cannot change the machine directly, nor do we wish to, once we understand its objective function as a transformational apparatus."

10) Ch. 6, "Beginning Work," Pg. 41

"We will also soon realize that in spite of its higher aims and aspirations, the essential self has no will in the ordinary sense, by which it can compel the machine to live according to its higher nature."

11) Ch. 6, "Beginning Work," Pg. 42

"So we must use what we actually do have in the essential self, the two genuine attributes of the essential self—presence and will-of-attention—to bring the machine into the waking state…"

12) Ch. 7, "Sheep in Sleep," Pg. 47

"We can use our attention to watch carefully and intensely everything the machine does…" [two paragraphs].

13) Ch. 7, "Sheep in Sleep," Pg. 48

"We quickly come to understand the sinister purpose of social ritual; we see how it helps to perpetuate the machine's sleep!"

14) Ch. 7, "Sheep in Sleep," Pg. 51

"Now, very softly, and in a very relaxed tone we will repeat…."

15) Ch. 7, "Sheep in Sleep," Pg. 52

"In our daily life, regardless of the circumstances in which we find ourselves immersed, we must try to actually obtain, and then hold, the sensation of the sleeping machine, at first doing nothing to awaken it directly."

16) Ch. 8, "Inner Aims", Pg. 57

"When we first come to a school, the question is put to us, why are we here, what do we wish for ourselves, what do we seek here, why do we impose ourselves on the community?"

17) Ch. 8, "Inner Aims", Pg. 60

"Our very first aim in a school will be a definite, objective school aim which we are expected to accomplish."

18) Ch. 9, "Study of the Machine," Pg. 78

"We will gather evidence of the machine's sleep for thirty days exactly...."

19) Ch. 10, "The Machine as an Electrical Field", Pg. 84

"Much of our ordinary muscle tension is the result of an overabundance of electrical force in the muscle. The tissue becomes tense as electrical resistance builds up."

20) Ch. 11, "The Repair of the Machine," Pg. 91

"Automatically as an experience is recorded in the muscles, the local electrical field is correspondingly altered."

21) Ch 13, "Help," Pg. 108

"Periodic emotional storms constantly serve as reminders that the machine has a will of its own."

22) Ch 13, "Help," Pg. 112

"The subtle force of our attention is our only weapon against sleep."

23) Ch. 15, "Bringing the Woman to Life," Pg. 130

"Now, in the same way, if we could view the human biological machine as a woman, as our initiator, our true teacher, and we could effectively place our restless, wandering attention completely upon it, the machine would come to life…"

24) Ch. 15, "Bringing the Woman to Life," Pg. 133

"By intentionally placing our unwavering attention directly upon the machine, and following its every motion with the emotional intensity of adoration, we develop a deep relationship with the machine."

25) Ch. 16, "Attack at Dawn: A Beachhead into the Fourth Dimension," Pg. 140

"…if we intend to try to awaken the machine, we must not do anything else at the same time. We must place a pure hermetic seal upon the time we have set aside for this effort…"

"Even with an untrained attention, anyone ought to be able to set aside five minutes a day during which nothing else enters to distract or attract the attention…"

26) Ch. 17, "Warming of the Soul," Pg 153

"We will imagine ourselves sitting cross-legged, holding a heavy ball of cold clay gently and lovingly in our cupped hands…"

27) Ch.18, "Out of Body," Entire Chapter, Pg 161

28) Ch. 19, "The Chronic Defense Mechanism," Pg. 173

"If we want to discover our chronic, all we have to do is go into horizontal sleep and have somebody shake us awake in the wee hours of the night or sometime in the pre-dawn and observe our first reaction. That will be our chronic."

29) Ch. 19, "The Chronic Defense Mechanism," Pg. 179

"Ritual and some forms of theatre, particularly mime, can actually help us to produce good habits of intentional reintegration of the sleeping state."

30) Ch. 20, "The Electrical Affinity of the Essential Self and the Machine," Pg. 190

"We are suggestible in the sense that one thing which seems similar to something else suggests that we include both in a fusion of synthesis, and categorize them together to save storage space in the memory sectors."

31) Ch. 21, "The Restimulation of the Defense Mechanism", Pg. 213

"At this point, we now turn back to a lower level of work and review some of the earlier material, but this time we do it in the waking state. ... We will scan to see if the sleeping state still has hooks, to see if there is anything left on machine levels."

32) Ch. 22, "Every Which Way But Up," Pg. 220

"Of course, as we put our attention on the machine and on the possibility of sleep, we know that the machine will awaken slightly. And if we can remember that the machine is in the sleeping state, we can be more alert to the potential for its awakening..."

Alphabetical Index

§

Dear Reader of *The Human Biological Machine....,*

The book which you have read is the first in a series of three practical books designed to offer explicit, straightforward, clear and easy to understand information issuing from a proven method of work-on-self.

The next volume in this Labyrinth Trilogy entitled *Life in the Labyrinth* is available in paperback and is recommended to those who are ready to go one step further in their efforts at work-on-self by broadening their vision and learning further applications of the ideas already expressed in this volume.

The third volume which the author recommends is his *Practical Work on Self,* a course of essence-attention exercises that lasts for six months to a year of hands-on work. These exercises may be carried out by the reader alone or in a discussion group setting, with a small group of associates who also apply the exercises.

Beyond these three volumes is an extensive course of work, including Bardo Training, spiritual gaming, attention and presence exercises, prescribed handicrafts, and much more. This work addresses those of us who are dissatisfied with the usual promises of enlightened self-gratification, simple emotional fulfillment, or personal enhancement. They speak to that part of ourselves which seeks to transform itself for the benefit of something higher.

We are pleased to be able to share this powerful work material with other seekers of the innermost path. For a current book catalog and information on further work materials, write to Gateways at the address shown below or check our website for the most current new releases in the Consciousness Classics series.

Gateways Books & Tapes
P.O. Box 370-HBM
Nevada City, CA 95959-0370

Phone: (530) 271-2239 or (800) 869-0658

Email: info@gatewaysbooksandtapes.com

Websites:
www.gatewaysbooksandtapes.com
www.idhhb.com
www.hei-art.com
www.talkofthemonth.com
www.brane-power.com
www.yoyodyneindustries.com
www.urthgame.com

Gateways Consciousness Classics
A Partial List of Titles You Can Order

Robert S. de Ropp

The Master Game: Pathways to Higher Consciousness
Self-Completion: Keys to a Meaningful Life
Warrior's Way: A Twentieth Century Odyssey

E.J. Gold

Alchemical Sex
American Book of the Dead
The Great Adventure: Talks on Death, Dying and the Bardos
The Human Biological Machine as a Transformational
  Apparatus
Practical Work on Self
The Hidden Work
The Seven Bodies of Man
Visions in the Stone: Journey to the Source of Hidden
  Knowledge (Intro. by Robert Anton Wilson)

Michael Hutchison

The Book of Floating: Exploring the Private Sea

Dr. Claudio Naranjo, M.D.

Character & Neurosis: An Integrative View
The Divine Child and the Hero: Inner Meaning in Children's
  Literature
The Enneagram of Society: Healing the Soul to Heal the World

The One Quest: A Map of the Ways of Transformation

Ka-Tzetnik 135633

Shivitti: A Vision

Dr. John C. Lilly

The Deep Self: Consciousness Exploration in the Isolation Tank
Tanks for the Memories: Floatation Tank Talks (with E.J. Gold)

Dr. Claude Needham, Ph.D.

The Original Handbook for the Recently Deceased
Just Because Club: Your Metaphysical Fitness Trainer
The Any Game Cookbook: Recipes for Spiritual Gaming

Mark Olsen

The Golden Buddha Changing Masks: An Opening to
Transformative Theatre

See www.gatewaysbooksandtapes.com for complete current
book list.